UNDERSTANDING THE ARAB WORLD

UNDERSTANDING
THE ARAB
WORLD

Louis Bahjat Hamada

THOMAS NELSON PUBLISHERS
Nashville

Published in Nashville, Tennessee, by Thomas Nelson,
Inc., and distributed in Canada by Lawson Falle, Ltd.,
Cambridge, Ontario.

Scripture quotations are from the NEW KING JAMES
VERSION of the Bible. Copyright © 1979, 1980, 1982,
Thomas Nelson, Inc., Publishers.

Library of Congress Cataloging-in-Publication Data

Hamada, Louis Bahjat.
    Understanding the Arab world / by Louis Bahjat
Hamada.
        p.   cm.
    Includes bibliographical references.
    ISBN 0-8407-3162-0
    1. Arabs in the Bible.   2. Arabs.   3. Hamada,
Louis Bahjat.
    4. Arabs—Missions.   5. Christianity and other
religions—Islam.
    6. Islam—Relations—Christianity.   7. Jewish-Arab
relations-
    -Religious aspects—Christianity.   8.
Terrorism—Religious aspects-
    -Christianity.   9. Protestantism and
Zionism—Controversial
    literature.   I. Title.
    BS680.A7H35   1990
    220.8′93949—dc20   90–6511
                                            CIP

Printed in the United States of America
1 2 3 4 5 6 7 — 95 94 93 92 91 90

Dedication

I dedicate this book to my people, the Arabs, for whom the Lord and Savior Jesus Christ also gave His life that He might redeem them from all iniquity, "and purify for Himself His own special people, zealous for good works" (Titus 2:14)!

The Arab world is made up of approximately 200 million individuals and most of them are Muslims. The rest are Christians, Druzes, and others. From West Africa to the Arabian Peninsula, Arabs remain the staunch guardians of the Muslim faith.

However, for several hundred years of evangelical Christian outreach, only a small number of Arab converts have been won for Christ and only a handful of struggling churches have been established. The reason for this deplorable situation will be discussed in the ensuing chapters.

To these converts and to Arabs from all walks of life and to their counterparts, this book is lovingly dedicated.

ALSO BY LOUIS BAHJAT HAMADA

God Loves the Arabs, Too

Contents

Acknowledgments   **ix**

Introduction   **xiii**

1   From Darkness to Light   **17**

2   The Semitic Arabs   **40**

3   God's Encounter with Hagar   **60**

4   Ishmael, Prince of the Desert   **84**

5   The Making of a Great Nation   **109**

6   The Arab World   **127**

7   Understanding the Arab Mind and Culture   **157**

8   A Christian Response to Arabic Terrorism   **176**

Notes   **192**

Subject Index   **196**

Scripture Index   **211**

About the Author   **215**

Acknowledgments

It is customary to list the names of the persons who have made the publication of a book possible. Some authors list many names, starting with their wives and children, and ending with the people who offered all kinds of help. However, no one stands higher than the blessed Person of the Holy Spirit, who has graciously constrained me and bestowed upon me the needed amount of illumination and guidance in the writing and completion of this long-awaited work.

This book has grown out of more than thirty years of biblical and cross-cultural studies. What is worth mentioning here is the fact that it took me less than four months to complete the writing of the manuscript. Ironically, I typed the whole work with my right forefinger (index finger), mainly because I was never interested in learning to type with both hands, nor was I interested in understanding the mysteries of the computer age and word processor. As one television commercial says, I "did it the old-fashioned way, I earned it."

The Lord gave me a strong desire to wake up every morning around 3 A.M., and enough strength to write at least fifteen hours per day. The writing took place during the stillness of the night and in the wee hours of the morning on my kitchen table, overlooking the backyard with its quiet atmosphere. I had my Bible, *Young's Analytical Concordance to the Bible*, an English dictionary, Webster's *New World Thesaurus*, and a few books and magazines to ferret out.

After praying for a short time, I have often felt like bursting from the joy of the Lord that flooded my soul. Suddenly, I began to unlock certain spiritual mysteries and visualize the things that I had not seen before. Ideas came to me gushingly, and their outflow revived my burdened heart and assured me that God was going to use my book to recondition the Western political theology of many Christian Zionists toward the Arabs, and also to use it worldwide for His evangelistic purposes.

I am indebted to my precious wife, Hanan, for writing a brief account about my upbringing—leading to my conversion to faith in Christ and ministry; and to my dear son and daughter, Omar and Sandy, who have been a great blessing and inspiration to me. I am also grateful to Thomas Nelson Publishers for encouraging me to write this timely volume and to Dr. Walton Padelford, president of the Hamada Evangelistic Outreach Ministries, who helped me proofread the manuscript.

May our dear Lord Jesus bless all those who would read this book. May they read it with an open mind, and may God use many of them to propagate the indiscriminate love of Christ, beginning "in Jerusalem, and in all Judea and Samaria, and to the end of the earth" (Acts 1:8)!

UNDERSTANDING THE ARAB WORLD

Introduction

In view of the magnitude of current crises in the Middle East, and because of the dire need to be more informed about the Semitic Arabs who carry great significance in the international balance of power, the writing of this book is both timely and relevant.

Of all the biblical peoples, the Semitic Arabs have received little consideration and study in modern times. Westerners seem to know little about Arab history, character, and culture. The rare courses about Arab peoples' sociological and historical background were limited to a few graduate schools and offered only under the small umbrella of Semitic studies. It was not until the recent turmoil between the Israelis and the Palestinians that the American government and public were awakened to the inescapable fact that there are more than a billion Arabs and Muslims with whom they have to deal diplomatically, and of whom they must have some understanding.

When I came to the United States from Lebanon as a student in 1953, I was excited to be in the land of opportunity and freedom. My fascination in discovering a new country and a new culture gave me great pleasure.

After a short time I realized that I had to adjust to a completely different life-style. I was unable to communicate my thoughts with my American friends and make myself understood. A familiar feeling came back to haunt me. This similar feeling strikes most foreigners, a feeling of loneliness and yearning to be with relatives and friends who share a kindred way of life and cherish similar customs and history.

I found myself reminiscing about past experiences and travels. The Western world's seeming inability and unwillingness to try to understand the Arabs bothered me. The public did not hold a positive and accurate image of our character and causes.

Many negative stories have been told about the Arabs, emanating from misperceptions and misunderstandings. I desire to help the reader understand the Arabs by presenting a fair portrait of them and stripping away some of the stereotypes that have led to so many misconceptions about this culture.

This book is a modest attempt to tell a short story of the Arabs and the Arabic-speaking peoples from early biblical times. The whole story cannot possibly be considered in a detailed fashion in one book; that would require a dissertation of encyclopedic proportions!

More specifically this book is written partly in answer to continual requests encouraging me to trace the origin and genealogy of Arabs, and partly to vindicate Hagar and Ishmael from the widely held mythical interpretations of Bible passages concerning them and their posterity. These timely requests have inspired and challenged me, providing the needed impetus to begin this long-awaited work.

Countless books and commentaries describe the biblical heritage of the Arabs from a negative point of view. These volumes have been unable to offer a true image of the Arabs' great contributions to our world in almost every field of knowledge. A good number of Western Arabists and analysts have built successful careers around studying the Middle East, without facing the fact that the Arab world is full of contrasts in cultural anthropology that seem to defy Western logic.

As far as I can determine, scarcely any systematic research has been done on God's historical use of the Arabs or on His indiscriminate love for them. The studies that have been made are inadequate and leave many questions unanswered, such as: Why are so many Western Christians provoking the Arabs to wrath by taking sides with Israel, and turning a deaf ear to the spiritual hunger of the Arabs? If Arabs have descended from Ishmael, as the popular and established belief teaches, why are they called Semites? What actually happened before and after God's encounter with Hagar? Did Ishmael become "a great nation," as God promised in Genesis 17:20? These and other pertinent issues will be discussed in the ensuing chapters.

The purpose of this informative and timely volume is to promote better understanding of Arabs and Muslims and to develop practical methods of sharing with them the unspeakable love of Christ. More than that, it is designed to help the reader gain an insight into the Arab culture and consider the hindrances to effective evangelism. This study should be useful not only to theological students, but also to a much wider range of readers. The reader may be surprised to discover new information that may recondition his or her views of anti-Arab bigotry that have been promulgated by Western political theology. Consequently, I feel compelled to offer a brief exposition of Arab history by drawing retrospectively on the conceptual scheme gained from personal study and cultural experience.

Since this book has grown out of a quasi-pioneering work, no attempt will be made to give full documentation. Sufficient biblical and extrabiblical sources for the little-known history and genealogy of Arabs will be included to substantiate the positions presented in this study. The study is not intended to be conclusive, but rather to provoke curious readers to conduct further research, as the Bereans did "daily to find out whether these things were so" (Acts 17:11). These acquired facts not only teach about God's divine election and historical use of Arabs, but also what they did and how they lived.

1

From Darkness to Light

Louis's story told by Hanan Hamada

"Summon all the children," Talal, the guard called out to the servants. "Take them to the bedside of Judge Mahmoud Bey."

It was daybreak when Bilhah the maid woke me up. The open windows in the two-story stone house welcomed the refreshing spring breeze. "Hurry up—put on your clothes, Bahjat," said Bilhah, "and come on—let us wash your face." Akāber, the other maid, was getting my younger sister, Aida, ready. I could hear them in the next room. Bilhah pulled me and raced toward my parents' room.

I was startled to see so many people, relatives, soldiers, and friends in the great living room, all sitting in great anticipation and anxiety. I wondered what was going on at such an early hour. Everyone seemed to look my way, and I could see sympathy for me in their eyes. When we got to the door of my parents' room, I ran inside. To my amazement, I saw my mother sitting at my father's side. My father was lying down on his bed struggling to breathe, as if his life were hanging by a thread.

A spirit of gloom and death hung over the room, and I

could see my mother's red and watery eyes. My father's gaze moved my way. Hanging onto the last moments of life, he gathered all his strength to open his arms to me, but my mother pulled me away and gently put me back close to him. He tried to hug me but was very weak. He then tried to speak, saying, "My son, take good care of yourself and grow up to be a man of integrity and courage. Take care of your mother and sister. May God bless you and bless your seed."

I kissed his hand and put it on my forehead so that he could bless me. I had learned as a young lad the importance of the parents' blessings, and I wanted my father to bless me. He looked at my mother and asked, "Souād, did the servant leave for Lebanon to bring Ismat and Sania?" (my older brother and sister who were in boarding school in Beirut.) She said, "Yes, he left during the night." Lebanon was two-days' journey away.

Mom pulled me to her side as my father started coughing blood. She called out to Bilhah and told her to take me back to my room and bring my sister, Aida, so she could see her father. I wanted to stay so much, but I knew I couldn't. After a few hours, I heard more noise and commotion in the house, and when I found out from the servants that my dad had just died, I became depressed and cried out for a long time.

We had to get ready to leave for Lebanon, to our hometown of Baakline, for Father's burial. That was a great shock to me, because my father seemed too young to die. My father had graduated from the Sorbonne School of Law in Paris, France. After he had earned his doctorate, the French government appointed him as prosecutor general at Hawran (biblical Haran), a southwestern district of Syria. Coming from a ruling aristocratic family of Lebanon, my father had been very much at ease with his position, and the people respected and honored him.

I could not imagine my father having any enemies; looking

in his soothing hazel-green eyes, I could see only compassion and love. I could not conceive of the fact that he was poisoned by his political enemies. At that moment in my life my heart was broken, and as a result, anger, hate, bitterness, and revenge filled my thoughts. I decided as a child of seven, that someday when I got older I would come back to take revenge for my dear father. That last farewell hung in my mind until we reached our mountain village of Baakline where the Hamada family palace was located.

People from Lebanon and different parts of the Middle East, France, and Britain, gathered in Baakline to bid their farewells and pay last respects to my father. As we stepped out of the car, a wail came out of my sister's servant. She ran to my mother to inform her that my baby sister, Aida, who was a chronic diabetic had died in her sleep, on the trip from Damascus. My mother and a few close relatives and friends took Aida in and checked her, but no response came from her. "We are going to have a double funeral for your father and your sister," Bilhah said.

I went into deep thought thinking to myself, "I wonder if we are cursed or something." In a few moments, we were joined by my older brother and sister, and together, we hugged and cried with bitter tears, as our hearts were overwhelmed with sadness.

My mother now was in mourning. According to our customs, she was supposed to go back to live in her parents' palace. Her father was the leader of the Druze religion in Lebanon, so she would be subjected to the moral ethics of that religion. My older brother and sister went back to their boarding school in Beirut while I stayed with my mother. I was now the focus of my mother's love and attention. I in return, being insecure and afraid to lose her, clung to her for dear life.

It was not long after, though, that my mother met a rich widower from the United States. He used to be from the

Hamada clan, working for them as a young lad. He always had in his heart to get to the top by marrying the daughter of one of the landlords. When he left for the States, he still kept that dream and worked hard to become a multimillionaire. After the death of his wife and the marriage of his oldest son, he came back to Lebanon seeking a wife. Knowing that my mother was available, he came to ask for her hand in marriage. Of course, Mother, steeped in a culture where the wife is faithful in life and death to one husband, would not even consider remarriage. After many consultations with her father and brothers, she finally agreed that it would be to her children's advantage to have a stepfather and come to the U.S. for our future learning.

After the marriage took place and it was time to leave for the U.S., my stepfather changed his mind about taking us with them. He promised, however, that after a short while he would bring us to live with Mom and him. That moment of separation was by far the most traumatic time of my life. It took all my uncles to pull my mother and me apart. I watched as she ascended the ladder to the ship. A feeling in my heart told me that this would be our last farewell. Here I was at age nine, left on my own it seemed. A week after my mother's departure, I signed all my inheritance away to my uncles as my legal guardians. They enrolled me in a Catholic boarding school for boys in Beirut.

A year later, we had news that my mother had died in a hospital in Flint, Michigan, while having her baby, a son. She and the baby died together in delivery. I found out years later that her death was not normal, but was inflicted on her and the baby by some relatives who wanted to appropriate my mother's inheritance. From a distant relative I learned that my mother's obstetrician had been bribed by some of the heirs to kill her and the baby. A few years ago I was in Flint and sought my mother's grave. After much searching I realized that she had been buried in an unmarked grave, to cover up the crime.

After my mother's death, I returned to the boarding school, where I felt abandoned and forsaken and very lonely. I did not like to study, so I spent my time daydreaming and fantasizing. Music and singing were my only comfort. My relatives discouraged my study of music, so it would not interfere with my academics. As a result, I kept my love for music a secret. I used to run away from school by climbing the high concrete wall. I used to cut my hands with the glass on top of the high wall and jump off in order to go to private music lessons. I studied voice and instrumental music, trying to learn the *oud* (a musical stringed instrument, the father of the guitar).

At age eighteen, one of my music teachers encouraged me to enter a voice competition at Radio Beirut. I entered the competition along with a great number of young people. I was very surprised when I made the finalists. At that time I became an aspiring singer. I saved every penny, and at age nineteen I bought a plane ticket to Egypt, and had some savings to take along.

Egypt was the Hollywood of the Middle East. I enrolled in the Egyptian conservatory of music and school of acting in Cairo to try my luck in show business. After two years I tried for a screen test—and to my surprise, I made it. I was able to act in a minor role in one movie with one of Egypt's most famous stars.

One day, however, I met a friend from my hometown in Lebanon. He was a very charismatic man. Most of those famous stars and singers were his friends. He promised that he could put me in touch with top stars—and I trusted in him.

One day he said he was in great need for cash. I had the amount he needed, so I offered him my money. Promising to pay me in a few days, he disappeared—and no trace of him could be found. As a result he tricked me out of all my money and left me penniless.

At that stage of my life I was so proud, I tried not to let anybody know of my need. I kept waiting for this man to come back, but he never did. I had very little to eat, so I stayed in bed most of the time. During this time, a well-dressed man approached me and put enough money in my hand to last me a week, then disappeared. He provided for me in this way for about a month. I was not able to ask him any questions it seemed. *Could he have been a messenger from God?* I wondered.

About a month went by, and my best friend from Lebanon, an air force pilot, flew his own private plane to Cairo to look for me. I'm sure God sent him to rescue me from illness. I was forever grateful and delighted to see him. He took me to his home in Beirut where he and his family nursed me back to health.

I went back to singing in Beirut, saved my money, and headed back to Egypt. I enrolled in the conservatory of music and the drama school of acting again, sang in private parties, in many movie stars' homes and night clubs, and was able to barely keep my head above the water. In 1952, the civil war broke out in Egypt, and King Farouk was dethroned and deported. Life became dangerous and I had to return to Beirut.

In 1953, I received a full tuition scholarship to the State Teachers College in Kirksville, Missouri. On June 5, 1953, I found myself on Pan American airlines leaving my beloved Lebanon. As the plane took off I felt my heart tearing within me as I was being uprooted to be transplanted to the West. When I arrived in America, the culture shock was overwhelming. I spoke Arabic and French, and English was not my language. I cried many nights, missing my friends and family. I had dreams of becoming a popular singer throughout the Lebanese American community in the entertainment field, but it was not easy. I looked for other jobs to help support myself, so I worked in the summers as a singing waiter in a summer resort in Maine and in the Grand Hotel on Mackinac Island, Michigan. I worked as a bellhop and entertainer singing in French, English, and Spanish. I sang in many conventions and clubs, and played my *oud* across the country. I saved my money in order to put myself through school.

On Friday, December 17, 1954, I was traveling to Carbondale, Pennsylvania, to spend the Christmas vacation with some friends. I was riding in the front seat of a 1951 Kaiser with four other students. We were on Highway 36, some four miles west of Chrisman, Illinois, which is located near the Indiana border. At 11:30 P.M. our car went into the back of a parked trailer truck taking the whole top of our car and killing all four of my friends. I woke up after two days in a coma to find out about the great tragedy and the fate of my friends. I wanted so much to die, but I could not take my own life.

In the spring of 1955, a criminal lawyer sought to use me as a witness to raise a case against the truck driver. He was hired by the parents of my deceased friends. When he found out that I had already signed a general release for the insurance company while I was in the hospital, he got very disgusted with me but he felt that he could not leave me alone. Being childless, he felt for me and took me with him to his home in New York.

After two months he took me to a ranch where a Christian missionary had a sort of youth camp on a farm in New Jersey, a ministry to win people to Christ. For ten days he preached Christ to me. I struggled in my soul with Christ and His claims to be God in the flesh. My religious upbringing had taught me to believe the greatest blasphemy was that God could be human. The Holy Spirit worked on me

23

very heavily and I finally surrendered my life to Him totally, turning from darkness to light. I was baptized the next morning with many other sinners identifying publicly with the Lord's death, burial and resurrection. The next day they put me on the Greyhound bus with twenty dollars in my pocket heading to Indianapolis, Indiana.

While I was performing for the Syrian-Lebanese Convention in French Lick, Indiana, I met the Dean of Butler University. After hearing me sing, he offered me a full tuition scholarship for Butler's school of music. I spent two years there studying vocal music. I pushed too hard trying to imitate Mario Lanza, so I damaged my vocal cords and developed nodes and had to be silent for six months.

In the fall of 1957, I transferred to the University of Miami, Florida. In Miami I sang in minor roles in the Opera Guild of Dade County. I graduated with a B.A. degree from the University of Miami in 1959.

After teaching at a private school in Miami for a year, I went to Tappahannock, Virginia in 1960 to start a high school band. I had to organize the band from scratch; the students had no musical background.

The *Richmond Times-Dispatch* newspaper, in the article of Monday, December 5, 1960, wrote "Back in September some 45 pupils turned out for the first band practice at Tappahannock High School. Not one of them could read a note and many did not know the names of most of the instruments."

The *Richmond NewsLeader*, state news, April 17, 1962, wrote, "Six months after organization, the band received a superior rating in the district band festival, a rating achieved by six of 24 bands competing."

In the *Richmond NewsLeader*, April 5, 1963, Dorothy Turner reported: "The Tappahannock High School band, in its third year of organization, had been chosen to be featured in 'The First Chair of America,' national band annual [the equivalent to *Who's Who* among high school bands]. Tappahannock was the only school in the state invited to appear in the 1963 edition."

The Lord already was the one who enabled me to succeed. I totally relied on Him and clung to Him for every aspect of my life. He directed my path as He promised He would do for them that obey Him and totally rely on Him.

In the summer of 1963, I attended the Domaine School of Conductors, in Hancock, Maine, to study under the supervision of the late gold-medal winner, Maestro Pierre Monteux. It was a great experience for me and it challenged me to continue for my graduate work in music.

In the fall of 1963 I enrolled in the graduate school of music at the University of Maryland at College Park. During that year a cousin of mine came to visit. He convinced me to go to Lebanon for a visit and also to seek a wife. In May 1964 I left my job and flew to Lebanon.

When I got to Lebanon I was met by my relatives and many friends in show business and the press. They were very happy to see me, so I had many TV, radio, newspaper, and magazine interviews. In the meantime I was meeting many girls from different walks of life and different religions. I also went with my uncle to meet many different Druze girls in their homes, according to the Druze tradition. At that stage of my Christian growth, I wanted to marry within my own culture. I could not seem to feel right about anybody, until I met Hanan. When I met Hanan I knew how precious she was. I fell for her and that night I could not sleep, but rather spent the night composing on my guitar a song called "Hanan."

Hanan was studying for her high school finals when I met her. She was aspiring to study medicine. The night I met her, however, I knew she was the one, the gift from the Lord for me. There were some difficulties and stumbling blocks to overcome for her father to agree to the marriage, but God worked it according to His sovereign plan, and we were married in two months.

We had a big, beautiful wedding according to the Lebanese tradition and spent our honeymoon in the Lebanese mountains. It was really very beautiful and very romantic. I hated for it to end. After a month, though, I had to leave for the U.S. to prepare the way for Hanan. Hanan could not come with me; she had to wait for her immigration papers and visa to the U.S. I stayed with my sister in Florida, and in the meantime applied for the graduate school at Florida State University.

Hanan came in September and we moved to Tallahassee, Florida. I started school at Florida State and in two-and-one-half years I graduated with a Ph.D. in Music Education. We had our son Omar while there in 1966. In the fall of 1967 we moved to Livingston, Alabama to teach choir and music education at Livingston University.

In 1968 we left for Lebanon to teach music in the schools in Lebanon. Before our departure, I acquired instruments of music and had them shipped in advance to Beirut. When I got there I was hired in the music department of the Beirut College for Women, The English School for Girls in Sidon, and the National Protestant School for Boys in Dubiyah, a suburb of Beirut. It took me a few months of walking every day miles at a time and going through unbelievable red tape in order to retrieve the shipped instruments out of the port. Corruption was everywhere in Lebanon; bribery was a way of life. I refused to bribe anyone, so I took the hard way out, and finally I was able to claim the instruments without paying a dime.

Music education was ignored in the public schools of Lebanon. The only music programs of even minimal significance were mostly transplants of the French and American systems in private schools. There was no indication of educational leadership in Lebanon for music education at either national or local levels, which was a genuine tragedy. Because of the media's enormous influence on national policy, I tried to convince them of the importance of music to the soul of man. I argued with them that with good music we find order, regularity, harmony, cohesion, balance, and proportion. Therefore, its role will influence the raising of stable character, training good citizens, and producing individuals with international culture. I argued that music is not only for the talented, but for integration into general education for everyone. I made my recommendations to the Lebanese Ministry of Education and showed them how important it was for children to be given equal opportunity for musical experiences and education. After a period of painstaking labor, my proposal was approved by the Ministry of Education.

In the schools in which I was teaching, I took the students who enrolled in music—and without them being able to read a note—we started a band in each school. We played a few concerts the first year, but we played for the general public the second year. We invited representatives of the Ministry of Education, school superintendents, principals, representatives of the Lebanese Conservatory of Music, and the press. After seeing and hearing the concert, music education became established in the schools of Lebanon.

While I was teaching in the Beirut College for Women, an American institution, I found out that the head of the religion department was a political agent, a member of a spy ring working undercover as a Christian missionary. He, and many others who went to the Middle East as wolves in sheep's clothing, had brought much damage to the spreading of the gospel and to the name of our dear Savior. I could not ignore this important issue, so I wrote a letter to the administration and faculty, exposing the evil motives of such people. I vindicated the name of our Lord and the true blessed missionaries that were there because of a deep commitment to the Lord and love for those people. In it I wrote, "The greatest contribution to come out of America has been the American missionary effort from which the B.C.W. was founded. . . . those selfless men and women who left the comfort and security of their homeland to bring the gospel of Christianity to the nations. . . . These missionaries have been far more effective ambassadors of goodwill than that of politics and other man-made objectives. . . . They represent the best of the original American dream: the self-lessness, the idealism. . . . In the late twentieth century, how-ever, a few young transitory immigrants have established themselves as teachers in Lebanese society that is steeped in culture and customs. Instead of fostering the original American dream they are seeking to destroy that dream. . . . We who had the good fortune of experiencing the help, goodness, goodwill, and democratic way of life of the Americans refuse to let a few troublemakers affect our youth with their deviousness, destroying the American image that we are striving to restore and foster."

After I distributed the letter to the faculty, I was repri-manded. I found out that some of the key members of the administration were also part of that spy ring. As a result, I was dismissed from my post, and we had to come back to the U.S. to find another job.

During that last year in Lebanon our daughter Sandy was born, and Hanan came to know the Lord Jesus as her Lord and Savior after experiencing pressure from circumstances and being drawn by the Holy Spirit. Leaving Lebanon again was not easy either for Hanan or for me. There we had our family and friends, our culture, our emotional ties, and our childhood memories. Lebanon at that time was breathtak-ingly beautiful. It had pleasant, mild weather, gorgeous na-ture, mixture of cultures, and a lot to offer in outdoor recreation and diversity of scenery, mountains, and the beach, the old and the new, the East and the West—all minutes from each other. Little did we know at that time that the Lord was pulling us out of Sodom—not to look back, but to look to Him and trust in His leading.

We reached New York in August 1970, leaving everything behind, including family, friends, country, and lots of valuable antiques and belongings. We were able to bring with us only two suitcases. We rented a small studio apartment in Mineola, Long Island, New York. We became sojourners again, starting a new life in our new country with our new faith.

Sure enough, the Lord had an ideal job waiting for me. I was hired as head of the instrumental music department at the Garden City Senior High School in Long Island, New York. The orchestra and concert band were already established and very professional. The instructor was taking a leave of absence for a year, and he wanted me to fill in for him. It was very refreshing to conduct this wonderful orchestra and concert band. I had a great rapport with my students and we enjoyed playing music together.

In March of that year I was getting ready to leave for a concert. As Hanan was preparing the children for the babysitter, she noticed that our son Omar, then almost five, was covered with bruises. She brought it to my attention and as a result we both felt that there was something very wrong with him. We rushed him to the emergency room of the Mineola Memorial Hospital. There we were told that Omar might have leukemia; he needed to stay in the hospital for further tests. We left brokenhearted and concerned.

Before the concert, I went to my office for a few minutes and cried my heart out. I begged God to touch my son and heal him. I promised the Lord that I would give a public testimony of His healing during the next concert. I went out with red and watery eyes to lead my orchestra. That night I conducted the whole concert from memory. The orchestra played its best and we had a long standing ovation. Glory to God; He did it again!

Omar had a very rare blood disease which was diagnosed as "Idiopathic Thrombocytopenic Purpura," which meant his platelet count got very low, his blood could not clot, and he bled internally. The doctors were unfamiliar with this disease and did not know how to treat it. On March 18, we passed through the valley of the shadow of death. Omar's platelet count dropped to rock bottom and the bleeding became extensive. He started hemorrhaging from his brain. The doctors told us that our son would probably not survive. Hanan and I knelt beside our bed and prayed earnestly that God would spare Omar's life, but we were willing to surrender him to Jesus. We went to sleep that night to be awakened by the doctor's call early in the morning. Omar's platelet count was normal. He did not understand but simply conveyed the news. The doctors expected the count to go down again, but we knew that our prayer had been answered. Jesus must have touched him and he was healed. At the same time, Omar also gave his little heart to Jesus.

April came and it was time for the spring concert. Omar was already healed with no trace of bleeding in his body. I remembered my promise to the Lord, to share publicly my testimony before the next concert. I was warned by my colleagues and friends not to share about what Christ had done, mainly because it was against the school policy to talk about Jesus. I ignored their warning and totally relied on Him. Before the concert I had Omar brought to the stage by one of my students. I took Omar by the hand and recounted the story to the 2,000 people in the auditorium and gave our Christian testimony, giving all the glory to our Lord Jesus. The whole auditorium broke into clapping and people stood up in honor for Christ. Weeks after, we saw people come to Jesus as a result.

In the fall of 1971, we moved to northern California to head the music department in a religious school. When I got there with my family, the school president gave us a house to stay in, a good salary, insurance, and many other benefits. It was not long though till we discovered that the place was a cult and that the president was a cult leader. She had swindled many people out of their finances, broken many homes, taken many children from their parents, and accepted praise from her followers—exalting herself and her three children above all. While she and her children were living in absolute luxury, her followers suffered severe financial hardships. All finances and assets of the followers were signed over to the cult leader and her children, including millions of dollars worth of real estate and large enterprises. We came to find out about her life of immorality with divorces and extortions.

One day while entering the school's church service, our eyes were drawn over the door to see the seal of the church. The seal showed the president sitting on the throne like a goddess with a scepter in her hand. We were shocked with all these facts, and staying there became unbearable. When she felt our hesitation to submit to her near-worship, she started threatening and putting us on the spot, using scary techniques, such as alienating us from that body of people. After a few months she pressured me to resign. She tried to break into our home and when she failed, then she cut off the utilities and gave us an ultimatum to leave the house in a few days. In the *New Yorker* magazine, the article "Annals of Crime," January 17, 1959, page 71, Bernard Taper writes about the husband of that cult leader saying, "he was found guilty of five counts. He was sentenced for seven years in prison, of which he served only three, before his release on account of a cardiac condition. During his stay in the penitentiary, his wife maintained the church and seminary . . . as she still does." Page 34 of that same magazine tells of their origin, "Both . . . had been born in rural Hickman County, Tennessee. . . . [He] was kicked out of school for making whiskey in the school basement. Later he was arrested in Florida on a charge of transporting stolen cars across the state line." In the spring of 1987 we were in that area speaking in a church. The pastor took us to their farm where bootlegging had taken place. This whole ordeal was one of the most trying trials in my life and the life of my family, and at the same time it was a great lesson in discerning sound doctrine. The Lord was faithful not to let us fall into that lie of deception. I can see how easy it is to be deceived and how people could be swayed to these different cults. By God's grace we came out and pulled out a few families with us. After we came out, my wife went to work and I started looking for a job. We wrote many schools in the south and the southwest parts of the U.S. One day we got two openings to choose from and after much prayer we took the one in Tennessee.

We moved our belongings and drove our car, which was not equipped with an air conditioner, through the desert and Death Valley in the middle of July. Needless to say, it was hot trying to cross the desert. When we got to Arizona I got very ill one night and had to be carried to the emergency room in the hospital in Winslow. It was the night of the prayer meeting of that cult, and I wondered if that had something to do with it. The Lord, however, sent me a Christian doctor and nurse who took care of me and prayed for my healing, and the second day we were on our way again to Tennessee.

When I got to the campus, I found that it was predominantly black. It was interesting to me because while in California, Hanan and I tried to go with some mission to Africa, but God never opened it. When I got here, however, I rejoiced because the college was truly my mission field.

I was hired as a full professor of music with tenure, and I taught the main courses in music appreciation and music education. That meant that every student had to take my course to graduate from college, and my classes were full. I set out to try to win my students to the Lord. Soon I found out that there was a racial problem in the South to such an extent that my students were rejecting "the white Christ" I was representing. One of my students was really radical and caused me much trouble, so I called him to my office to see what was the problem. I came to find out that many churches erroneously taught that the blacks were cursed according to the Bible, and therefore they were to be subservient to the whites. I was shocked to discover this and to find that most of my white friends believed it. As a result, I enrolled in Dallas Theological Seminary to expose this wrong teaching that was keeping my black friends from the gospel of truth. Dallas Seminary appealed to me because it is interdenominational, and it stands for biblical inerrancy.

In the summer of 1976, I enrolled in the Dallas Theological Seminary for the graduate program M.A.B.S. I attended during summers, Christmases, and every vacation I had. I studied very hard in every empty minute. After two years I wrote my thesis on Noah's curse on Canaan, which was a prophetic curse on the land and *not* the people.

I came back to Tennessee with such freedom to explain God's indiscriminate love to my students. I came to see hundreds of my students get the vision and follow the Savior as a result. It was so exciting that I needed help to disciple the many that came. My white Christian friends did not seem excited, however, and did not care to have the black students come to their churches, so I discipled them on campus. I went two nights a week. On Wednesday I taught on God's love, and on Friday I taught on God's wrath, to give them a good healthy diet of the gospel. My students started growing in Christ and a few leaders surfaced. Hypocrisy was rampant in the churches and those religious Pharisees were and still are refusing to see the heart of our Savior that sees the world with equal compassion. In my ninth year my beloved students started opening their hearts to me and airing their griefs. They shared with me concerning the immorality that was saturating the college, such as homosexuality, promiscuity, sex orgies, and other destructive humanistic practices that were forced on the students, sometimes for grades.

The Lord did not let me sleep nights; He kept putting on my heart to do something about these problems. My white Christian friends discouraged me, saying that I might get hurt in the process. One day after talking with my wife during our prayer time, the Lord led us to Jeremiah 1:7b–10, 17: "'For you shall go to all to whom I send you, and whatever I command you, you shall speak. Do not be afraid of their faces, for I am with you to deliver you,' says the Lord. . . . 'Behold I have put My words in your mouth. See, I have this day set you over . . . to root out and to pull down, to destroy and to throw down, to build and to plant.' . . . 'Therefore prepare yourself and arise, and speak to them all that I command you. Do not be dismayed before their faces, lest I dismay you before them.'"

I obeyed the Lord and wrote a letter to the administration and all the faculty. In the letter I besought them to listen to God's voice and turn away from their wicked practices. Shortly after, I was called on the carpet before the whole board of the school. It is interesting to note that the only one who stood by my side publicly regarding this moral issue was a Muslim who agreed with me wholeheartedly, while some Christians were afraid and kept silent. One board member said, "Maybe where you come from, in Lebanon, it is wrong to practice homosexuality, but definitely not here."

I was asked to resign after this meeting, even though I had tenure. I could have sued the school for losing my job, but I left in peace trusting my Lord for my future.

I had a friend, a pastor of a church in southern California. One day I called him to talk to him about my situation. He felt he could use me in his church if I would come by faith expecting no pay from his church. Before my departure, God gave me Mark 10:29–30: "Assuredly, I say to you, there is no one who has left house or brothers or sisters or father or mother or wife or children or lands, for My sake and the gospel's, who shall not receive a hundredfold now in this time—houses and brothers and sisters and mothers and children and lands, with persecutions—and in the age to come, eternal life." I left knowing He who called me would lead me and take care of me and my family.

When I got to southern California, the need was great. I stayed in different homes of the church members and had a small office in the church. I started nightly Bible studies in different homes for discipleship and growth. I also had a ministry of counseling. Many church members came and brought others with them. The Lord brought people from all walks of life, backgrounds, and nationalities. The police department brought high school delinquent students for help. I came to see many people accept Christ. Their lives were transformed by the power of the Holy Spirit and the Word, many homes were healed, many sins forsaken, and many Christians were restored to faith. I dealt with all kinds of problems, such as drug addiction, homosexuality, criminal behavior, demon-possession, marital conflicts, and so forth. Because of the numerous cults in that area, I was asked to teach on the various cults and false doctrines. I had a series of lessons on each cult; many wrong doctrines were exposed. When I began teaching on Freemasonry, however, I felt strong opposition from the church leadership. I was advised to stop teaching and leave the church as soon as possible. The elders of the church belonged to that group, and they did not want it exposed. I did leave and went back to Tennessee to see what the Lord had for me to do.

That summer the Lord took me to West Germany to teach in a conference for converted Muslims. One night I taught on the cost of discipleship. After the meeting, a German friend, the head of a West German mission, called me to his office. "Dr. Hamada, did you mean what you taught tonight?"

"Of course," I blurted out, "I meant every word."

"Then how about going to Israel in the morning, on a mission to evangelize our friends the Arabs?"

Abruptly, I said, "No, I am not interested, thank you."

"What if God wants you there?"

"I will think about it," I immediately answered.

Israel had invaded Lebanon at that time; it was dangerous for a Lebanese to be in Israel. I also knew I would be misunderstood by my brothers, the Arabs. Carrying many past wounds of persecution, I was reluctant to be misinterpreted. I left my friend's office, quietly arguing with God and telling Him that He could not want me to go to Israel. Of all places, that was the last place I wanted to be. I wanted nothing to do with the Arabs, especially evangelizing them. When I tried to sleep, however, the Lord started talking to my heart about the Arabs. He started pulling out roots of bitterness and revenge that I carried in my heart for years. Consequently, the Lord broke my heart for my people and I was ready to go. The next morning my German friend had my tickets ready and I found myself on the plane going to Israel. I was a Lebanese with an American passport coming alone.

On the plane, the Lord put a young Lebanese student next to me. He was going to visit his parents in Sidon. We talked all the way from Frankfurt to Tel-Aviv. Before we landed, my friend gave his life to Christ. When we got there, my friend underwent a severe scrutiny and he had to be stripped naked and searched, very humiliating indeed. In my case, however, because of my American passport it was much easier. They took me to a room with secret police and questioned me for a long time before they released me. "Where are you going?" "I do not know," I answered. "Where will you be staying?" "I do not know," I answered again. "Why are you here?" "On a mission." "Aha," they said and looked at each other, thinking they caught a big fish. "What kind of a mission?" they questioned. "I am coming to evangelize the Arabs," I said. "Good, go evangelize them, but make sure to leave the Jews alone. It is against the law to proselytize a Jew." "Fine with me," I said to myself, thinking, "What hypocrisy! They use the American Christians to send them money as long as the gospel is kept out of Israel."

I went on my way, trusting God to lead me in the way I should go. A secret policeman was watching me, but I had nothing to hide, so I did not worry and I went my way. The Lord led me to Nazareth, and while there I met a very nice Palestinian, well-dressed and well-educated. We became good friends and we met for coffee for a few days. He happened to be a Muslim, and he knew what I had in mind being there. He brought his Qur'an, and I brought my Arabic Bible, and he started questioning me. "Was Jesus a Jew?" "Yes, He was," I answered. "Was He God?" "Yes, He is, of course," I said assuredly. "Then, you are saying to me that God is a Jew." "No, of course not." "What do you mean? You just told me that Jesus is a Jew, and He is God, so therefore, you are saying: God is a Jew." Then he left that and went to Galatians 4:30, as he heard it preached from many TV evangelists. He said, "According to your Bible we are cast out, aren't we?"

"No, of course not," I confidently said.

He recounted to me how often he had heard American

preachers and evangelists say that God cast out Hagar and Ishmael, and those who curse the Jews will be cursed (Gen. 12:3). I left brokenhearted, defeated, and humiliated. I went to my room and sobbed before God and told Him, "Did I not tell You? I do not want to come here. What a mistake. I can not even defend You and Your character. I do not want to be a missionary, but I do want to go back to teach music." All night, however, I tossed and turned as if hearing God tell me "Who will I send and who will go for Us?" after much struggle I said "OK, Lord. Here I am. Send me."

Later on a brother and sister in Christ had us in their home to pray. They prayed and shared with us about starting a faith ministry to the Arabs. A few days later God spoke to another brother in Christ who was preparing his Sunday school lesson. While he was sitting under his tree in his backyard, the Lord led him to 3 John: 5–8, "Beloved, you do faithfully whatever you do for the brethren and for strangers, who have borne witness of your love before the church. If you send them forward on their journey in a manner worthy of God, you will do well, because they went forth for His name's sake, taking nothing from the Gentiles. We therefore ought to receive such, that we may become fellow workers for the truth."

He called me that day and shared with me his desire to start this ministry. In seven weeks the Lord had seven men on the board and the ministry was started. In seven months after the Lord had launched this ministry, He took us across the U.S., Europe, and the Middle East. We saw many Arabs come to know Christ from various religions and different countries. The Lord was bearing witness and showing His approval on this ministry by saving many, such as my brother.

The Lord then put on my heart to write my first book about the Arabs and His love for them, dealing with all the questions that my friend the Palestinian asked me in Israel.

Consequently, God clarified our calling which is to expose the Western political theology, to recruit and train missionaries using only the biblical approach for evangelism, and showing the Arabs God's indiscriminant love and their place in God's plan for the ages.

2

The Semitic Arabs

While there are differences of opinion among Bible scholars and historians as to the origination of the Arabs, the most authoritative record in existence which accurately traces them to their true lineage is the Torah, or more precisely, the Book of Genesis.

Most Westerners would be surprised to learn that Arabs and Jews originated from the very same parents, and that both of them are called Semites, mainly because they were both descendants from the only two sons of Eber. Eber literally refers to the people living "over the other side," or "beyond the river [Euphrates]."[1] *Abir* is the Arabic word for Eber, meaning "to cross over."

Eber was a great-grandson of Shem, one of the three sons of Noah (Gen. 10:1, 22, 24). Eber had two sons, Peleg and Joktan. The Arabs descended from Joktan; the Hebrews from Peleg. Peleg means division, "for in his days the earth was divided" (Gen. 10:25).

Etymologically, the term *Arab* is a Semitic word derived from the Hebrew *Eber,* meaning "desert." In the Qur'an, the Muslims' holy book, the word *Arab* is used for Bedouins, denoting "nomads." One of the early biblical uses of the word *Arab* as a proper name occurs in Jeremiah 25:24, "kings of Arabia." These kings were probably sheikhs or heads of tribes living near the Arabian Peninsula and the Syrian Desert.

According to a Hebrew and Chaldee dictionary, *Arab* comes from a primary root word meaning "to lie in wait, to mingle and intermix, to give or be security, to engage and meddle with, to undertake close association, to be pleasant, to grow dusky at sundown, to be darkened toward evening." This statement briefly describes some of the characteristics of the nomadic life-style of Arabs.

The terms *Arabah* and *Arabia* simply refer to "the plain, or wilderness."[2] The Arabs and Hebrews originally did not comprise either a nation or nationality. They were nomadic tribes wandering in the wilderness. The nature of the desert forced them to roam from one water source to another, seeking pasture to feed their flocks.

Ironically, the word *Semite* has come to possess an exclusive Jewish connotation in the Western world. Because of their historical dispersions and their intermarriage with the Gentiles, the Jews have not maintained their ethnic purity. On the other hand, the Arabs may be considered the best representatives of the two surviving "Semitic families biologically, psychologically, socially and linguistically."[3] The Arabs have been able to preserve their cultural traits due to their monotonous uniformity of sedentary desert life.

More often than not we are told that Abraham was a Jew. The word Jew, *Yehudi* in the Hebrew, refers to those descended from Judah, one of the twelve sons of Jacob (Gen. 29:35). Abraham was the first person to be called "the Hebrew" (Gen. 14:13), meaning "one from the other side."[4] The term was used at that time as a general designation for ethnic people who had lived a nomadic life like Abraham. It also had a wider meaning since Abraham was considered by the Canaanites a migrant from Ur (modern Iraq) and Haran, a southwestern district of Syria.

Abraham, Sarah, and all their relatives were not Jews— they were Gentile pagans from "Mesopotamia" (Acts 7:2), who served "other gods" (Josh. 24:2). They were called Hebrews because they descended from Eber (Gen. 11:16–26). William Whiston, who translated the complete works of Flavius Josephus, stated:

> That the Jews were called Hebrews, from this their progenitor Heber, our author Josephus here rightly affirms; and not from Abram the Hebrew, or passenger over Euphrates, as many of the moderns suppose. Shem is also called the father of all the children of Heber, or of all the Hebrews, in a history long before Abram passed over Euphrates (Gen. xiv. 13) where the original says they told Abram the Hebrew, the Septuagint renders it the passenger. But this is spoken only of Abram himself, who had then lately passed over Euphrates: and is another signification of the Hebrew word, taken as an appellative, and not as a proper name.[5]

The Joktanites

Long before Abraham was born, the Arabs descended from Eber through Joktan, or "Kahtan" as they prefer to call him. Joktan comes from the Hebrew word meaning small in stature. A derivative word of Kahtan is *kaht*, denoting drought. Joktan fathered the thirteen Arabian tribes of Genesis 10:26–29. Their original boundaries were stated in the Word of God: "And their dwelling place was from Mesha as you go toward Sephar, the mountain of the east" (Gen. 10:30).

Following is a brief description of the Joktanite tribes and their boundaries. Mesha is located toward the western boundary of the Arabian Peninsula. It was a desert district

The Joktanites

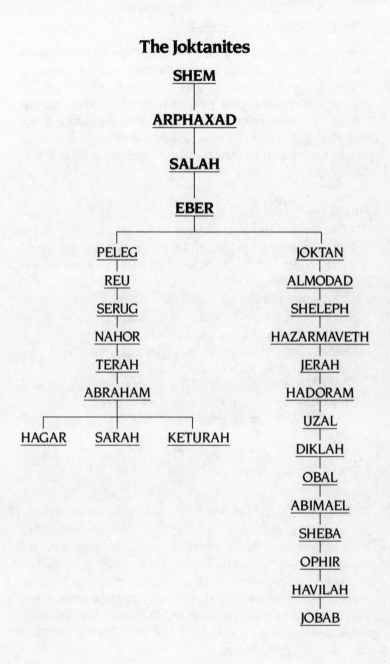

SHEM

ARPHAXAD

SALAH

EBER

PELEG   JOKTAN

REU   ALMODAD

SERUG   SHELEPH

NAHOR   HAZARMAVETH

TERAH   JERAH

ABRAHAM   HADORAM

HAGAR   SARAH   KETURAH   UZAL

DIKLAH

OBAL

ABIMAEL

SHEBA

OPHIR

HAVILAH

JOBAB

stretching from west to east toward Sephar (Zhafar), which was a seaport east of Yemen. A great trade was carried on in ancient times with Africa and India from this seaport. "The Yemen embraced originally the most fertile districts of Arabia, and the frankincense and spice country. Its name signified 'the right hand.' This describes the country's position as one faces the east toward the Kaaba in Mecca, Su'udi Arabia."[6]

Almodad—The Beloved

Almodad was the eldest son of Joktan. His name appears to be preserved as Mudad or El-Mudad, meaning the friend of God. According to Ibn-Khal-dūn (1332–1406), recognized as the greatest Arabian historian, Almodad was the reputed father of Ishmael's Arab wife, Mir-āt ez-Zaman. Ishmael's mother, Hagar, took her as a "wife for him from the land of Egypt" (Gen. 21:21). Egypt was founded by Mizraim, the second son of Ham (Gen. 10:6), and Egypt is called "the land of Ham" (Pss. 105:23; 106:22).

The Arabs are still being called the sons of Kahtan, and they affiliate Almodad's descendants with the tribe of Morad. This tribe apparently feared the God of Shem and worshiped Him. The people were reported to be very friendly and hospitable, especially to strangers. They lived in a mountainous region of Arabia.

Sheleph—Drawn Out

This second son of Joktan has been identified by Arab historians as the tribe of Shelif or Shulaf, belonging to the Yemen. His name in Arabic is Salafa, meaning to cultivate or to pluck out. The name corresponds to farming or to cultivating the ground and planting in order to raise crops. Sheleph may also mean to promote or to devote oneself to seek the acquaintance or friendship of others. The modern descendants of this tribe are found in the southern district of Selfia.

Hazarmaveth—Village of Death

The name Hazarmaveth is preserved in the province of southern Arabia, east of modern Yemen. Hazarmaveth is *Hadramawt* in Arabic. Its capital city is Shibam, and its chief seaports are Mirbat, Zhafar, and Kisheem—from whence a great trade was carried on in ancient times with India and Africa. "Hadramawt, on the coast east of the Yemen, is a cultivated tract contiguous to the sandy deserts called El-Ahkaf, which are said to be the original seats of the tribe of Ibn-El-Wardee. It was celebrated for its frankincense, and formerly it carried on a considerable trade with near and far away nations. Its principal port being Zafari, between Mirbat and Ras Sajr, which is now composed of a series of villages."[7]

Jerah—Moon

The moon held a very important place for the Arabian tribe Jerah, probably because it gave the poets great inspiration and provided the ambiance for meditation. It has been said that since the moon was appointed "to rule the night" (Gen. 1:16), its worship was practiced by many ancient tribes and nations. The tribe of Jerah lived near the Red Sea and Yemen.

Hadoram—Hadar Is Exalted

Hadoram was the fifth son of Joktan, and probably merged with Hazarmaveth and became known as Hadramawt. Other than that, very little is known about this tribe.

Uzal—Beautiful Trees

The ancient capital of Yemen was called Uzal or Awzal. The name was later changed to San'a. This tribe planted beautiful trees and was highly developed technically as witnessed by the remains of a great dam at Mārib, east of San'a, which became the center of a large irrigation system. The dam held and controlled the water rushing down from seventy mountain peaks. It was destroyed and rebuilt three times before its final destruction in the sixth century A.D.

Diklah—Palm Tree

The original Arabic word *diklah* means a palm tree abounding with fruit. Usually the heart of an ordinary tree is dead, but the heart of the palm tree is alive because the life of the palm tree is on the inside. It was created so outward abuses do not affect its quality of fruit. Strong desert winds and heat ordinarily can destroy other trees, but the palm tree patiently endures and bows to the ground and springs back and stands tall when the heat and winds subside.

Palm trees not only withstand abuse and endure storms, but they are also able to survive drought by sending their roots deep into the ground to tap necessary resources of nourishment. Usually palm trees need at least fifty years to mature and bear fruit (dates). As they grow older, their fruit grows more delicious and sweet.[8]

I believe this has been the historical character of most Arab tribes, and these characteristics have been passed on to their posterity. Generally speaking, most Arabs are sweet in disposition, engaging, kind, generous, good humored, and friendly. They have been given the ability to withstand abuses and endure suffering under the most grueling circumstances. They were created wild (meaning extravagant and unable to be tamed by coercion) because God has made them free-spirited, and no one has been able to uproot them from their homeland (Gen. 16:12).

The palm tree is a symbol of patience, endurance, and prosperity. These traits were bestowed upon Diklah's descendants who settled in Yemen, alongside their brethren, and occupied a part of central Arabia, notably in Nejd and Hijaz, along the northeast coast of the Red Sea.

Obal—To Be Bare

In 1 Chronicles 1:22 Obal is called Ebal, meaning arid and stony. Probably this Arabian tribe did settle in an extremely barren land from lack of moisture. Little is known about this tribe. According to the Bible, God put a curse on some Israeli tribes who had lived in the Samarian hills of Mount Ebal because they violated His commandments. Also, Joshua built an altar there and a monument inscribed with the Law of Moses (Deut. 11:29; 27:4, 13; Josh. 8:30–33).

Abimael—God Is Father

Abimael was the founder of the Arabian tribe called Mael or Mali. In a broader sense, Abimael could be translated "father of a king," or "father-king." The Arabs had many heads of tribes called kings: "all the kings of Arabia and all the kings of the mixed multitude who dwell in the desert" (Jer. 25:24).

Many non-Arab tribes called their kings Abimelech. The Philistine king of Gerar who tried to take Sarah into his harem was called Abimelech (Gen. 20:2). Another king of Gerar in the time of Isaac was called Abimelech (Gen. 26:1). This king was supposed to have been the son of the first Abimelech. Also the king of Shechem was called Abimelech (Judg. 9:22).

Sheba—Seven; An Oath

Sheba was one of the most important sons of Joktan and a grandson of the patriarch Eber. His tribe colonized southern Arabia and became known as the kingdom of Sheba, or the kingdom of the Sabeans. This kingdom embraced a vast part of Yemen and was greatly blessed with gold, frankincense, and myrrh. These same gifts were given to the Christ child, and they are held to be the kinds of gifts Abraham had given to his six sons through Keturah (Gen. 25:6). The Queen of Sheba presented these same gifts to King Solomon when she came to hear his wisdom (1 Kings 10:1–10). In a psalm foreshadowing the Messiah, the gift of Arab gold was foretold: "And He shall live; And the gold of Sheba will be given to Him; Prayer also will be made for Him continually, And daily He shall be praised" (Ps. 72:15).

It is believed that the Sabeans migrated south and colonized Ethiopia around the tenth century B.C., at the same time the Queen of Sheba, called "Balkis" by the Arabs, visited King Solomon and exchanged valuable presents with him. The Lord Jesus spoke of her as the "Queen of the South" (Matt. 12:42). I believe that many descendants of the Semitic Arab tribes worshiped the "God of Shem" (Gen. 9:26).

The kingdom of Sheba was near the trade route from India to Africa and was known for its great wealth. It was also a social and political center. Its culture reached an unprecedented height from about the sixth to the fifth century B.C. Many inscriptions were found in Sheba showing great engineering works.

Ophir—Rich

Josephus (A.D 37–95.), the renowned Jewish historian, and the Septuagint identify Ophir with India. Sophir, or Sophira, is the name used by Josephus. *Sofir* is the Coptic word for India. Also, Arabian historians translated the word *Ophir* as India. In other words, the descendants of Ophir colonized India and opened a trade route toward Arabia and Africa.

The Bible describes Ophir as very rich with gold, precious stones, and spices (1 Kings 9:28; 10:11; Isa. 13:12). Some say that Ophir's location is unknown. Others identify it with Yemen, which was famous for gold production and prominent in the Old Testament. Solomon's ships brought from Ophir "gold . . . and precious stones" (I Kings 10:11).

Havilah—Circle

It is commonly thought that the district of Khawlan in Yemen was the location of Havilah. Khawlan is located between San'a and Hijaz in the northwestern section of Yemen. The district of Khawlan is a fertile territory with plenty of water. God created a river to water the Garden of Eden. One of the "four riverheads. . . . encompasses the whole land of Havilah, where there is gold. And the gold of that land is good" (Gen. 2:10–12).

Jobab—Howling

One of the kings of Edom is called Jobab (Gen. 36:33). The Septuagint identifies him as the patriarch Job, whose father was Zerah, a descendant of Esau. The Arabic word for Job is *Ayyoub*. Interestingly enough, Job is considered by many biblical scholars and historians as an Arab. "Job, the author of the finest piece of poetry that the ancient Semitic world produced, was an Arab."[9]

It is believed that Job lived in the region of Damascus during the nineteenth century B.C., around the time Jobab settled between Syria and Palestine. According to the Bible, Job was living in the land of Uz (Job 1:1) during that time, which can be traced between Edom and Damascus, probably the same location and the same period of Jobab's settlement.

God gave Joktan thirteen sons, whose names were recorded in Genesis 10:26–29 and in I Chronicles 1:20–23. They were blessed with much lands and great wealth. More than that, these Semitic Arabs withstood the abuses of nature and peoples and enjoyed the unmatched beauty and freedom of desert life.

The Ishmaelites

ABRAHAM AND HAGAR

ISHMAEL

NEBAJOTH

KEDAR

ADBEEL

MIBSAM

MISHMA

DUMAH

MASSA

HADAR

TEMA

JETUR

NAPHISH

KEDEMAH

The Ishmaelites

Ishmael was the eldest son of Abraham by Hagar. After Abraham's intercession on behalf of his son, God said: "And as for Ishmael, I have heard you. Behold, I have blessed him, and will make him fruitful, and will multiply him exceedingly. He shall beget twelve princes, and I will make him a great nation" (Gen. 17:20). Here are the twelve princes of Ishmael.

Nebajoth—Husbandry

Nebajoth was the eldest son of Ishmael and the founder of the tribe of Nabat. The Nabat became known as the Nabathaeans who were neighbors to the Arabian clan of Kedar (Isa. 60:7). Nebajoth or Nebaioth and his tribe inhabited the land *beyn-en-nahrein,* between the Tigris and Euphrates, the Mesopotamia and Chaldea of ancient times. The Arabs apply the name Nabat to Syria. According to Arabian history, the Chaldaeans and Nabataeans were the same as the Syrians. The Arabian historian El-Mes'oudee contends that "the Syrians are the same as the Nabataeans." They were also called Syro-Chaldaeans. The Nabataeans founded the city of Babylon, and the inhabitants of Nineveh were called Nabeet, or Syrians. They were "a pastoral people with great knowledge of agriculture, astronomy, medicine, science, and the arts."[10] It is assumed that the Chaldaeans sprang from Nebajoth through intermarriage with Cushite groups.

The Nabataeans were very gifted people. They built reservoirs, dams, and aqueducts in Sela, northwest of Buseirah, identified in the Bible as Bozrah, Iraq (Isa. 63:1). They developed a great civilization, and Petra's fortress became their habitat when they gained control of the caravan routes during the sixth and fourth centuries B.C. Petra was known at that time as Sela in the Old Testament (2 Kings

14:7; Isa. 16:1). "Petra was generally known as the land of Edom, or Idumaea, as well as by its other appellation, the desert of Seir, or Mount Seir. It is commonly believed that the Idumaeans descended from Esau and Mahalath, Ishmael's daughter" (Gen. 28:9; 36:9)."

The Judaean king, Herod the Great, had Nabataean blood infusion through intermarriage. His father, Antipater, was Idumaean, and his mother was of Nabataean origin. His son, Herod Antipas, married the daughter of Aretas IV, king of the Nabataeans, who ruled from 9 B.C. to A.D. 40.

Kedar—Dark

The tribe Kedar was comprised of skilled archers and fierce fighters. Kedar settled on the northwest part of the Arabian Peninsula and the confines of Palestine (Isa. 21:13–17). Ezekiel declares that the princes of Kedar were Arabian merchants. "They traded with you in lambs, rams, and goats" (Ezek. 27:21). The people lived in black tents made of camel's hair or black goatskin. In Arabic they are called *beit sha'ar,* meaning house of hair. The Hebrew word for beit is *bavith,* literally denoting shelter. The English equivalent is house or home. Hitti postulates that the Shulamite woman in the Song of Solomon was the beautiful "Queen of Sheba."¹² Solomon compares her attractive complexion with "the tents of Kedar" (Song 1:5).

Adbeel—Disciplined of God

Adbeel is said to be the twenty-first generation before the birth of the prophet Muhammad. Other than that, I was unable to ferret out more worthwhile information about him.

Mibsam—Sweet Odor

The word *balsam* is derived from Mibsam. Balsam is a fragrant resin obtained from a variety of trees. Some balsams contain cinnamic acid or benzoin and storax, which can be found in South America and probably in the Middle East. Other balsams include the Mecca balsam of Saudi Arabia. In addition to perfumes, balsams are also used in medical preparations.

According to Arabian history, this tribe settled in the district of Mecca, and balsam was used extensively to give surroundings a fresh fragrance.

Mishma—Hearing

Mishma means hearing or report. Arabian tradition asserts that the Masamani tribe, called Beni-Misma, spent their time telling fables and reporting current news. This has been a characteristic of tribal social activity. The Masamanis were very hospitable people, but this kind of unproductive habit has been passed on to other cultures, such as the Greeks. "For all the Athenians and the foreigners who were there spent their time in nothing else but either to tell or to hear some new thing" (Acts 17:21).

The Masamani tribe lived in the province of Arabia, neighboring the tribe of Mibsam and not far from Mecca.

Dumah—Silence

Dumah was an Arab village neighboring "the cities at the limits of the tribe of the children of Judah, toward the border of Edom in the South" (Josh. 15:21, 52; cf. Isa. 21:11). Wilhelm Gesenius (1786–1842), a Jewish scholar, said that Dumah settled in Doomat-el-Jendel in the northwestern region of Arabia. "Dumat al-Jandal (modern al-Jawf) is situated midway between al-Iraq and Syria."[13]

Massa—Burden

Massa was the progenitor of the Massani tribe who lived in eastern Arabia, near the border of ancient Babylonia. In

Proverbs 30:1, some hold the proper reading to be "Agur the Massite," who lived in the area of the Massani tribe. Others maintain the reading to be the "Lemuel" of Proverbs 31:1. Hitti said, "Agur the son of Jakeh (Prov. 30:1) and of Lemuel (Prov. 31:1), the two kings of Massa, a tribe of Ishmael (Gen. 25:14)."[14]

Hadar—Fierceness

Hadar, or Hadad, lived near the borders of the Syrian desert. This tribe should not be identified with the Hadad who descended from Esau. The Edomite Hadad was a prince who escaped Joab's massacre by fleeing to Egypt, marrying the Pharaoh's sister-in-law, and returning to rescue Edom from Solomon's oppression (1 Kings 11:14–25).

Tema—Sunburnt

Tema settled between Damascus and Mecca. Cuneiform inscriptions have been discovered from Tema, *Tayma* in Arabic, which is a large oasis in southwest Saudi Arabia. Arabic tradition tells us that the oasis was very rich in water and beautiful buildings. Job spoke of this tribe in parabolic fashion (Job 6:19), and Isaiah 21:14 mentioned the good deeds of Tema toward the hungry and thirsty, describing Arab generosity.

Jetur—Nomadic Camp

Jetur was the founder of Ituraea, an ancient country bordering the northern part of Palestine. The Arabians inhabited the country with their capital city at Chalchis and had their religious center at Heliopolis (modern Baalbek in Lebanon).

Baalbek brings back beautiful memories for me. After I earned a doctorate degree in music education from Florida State University, I took my family to Beirut in 1968, intending to use my skills in my native country. I will not forget how excited I was when the Lebanese Ministry of Tourism asked me to translate from English to Arabic, the story of "Spartacus" and explain it to the public on national television. "Spartacus" was a ballet set to music by Aram Khatchatourian, a Russian composer of Armenian extraction.

On account of my labor, my wife and I were invited to attend the ballet, which was performed in the open air at the ancient theater of Baalbek. A group of dancers and musicians from Budapest gave a memorable presentation to a full house of music lovers. The moon was shining brightly and permeated the two courtyards of the temple ruins, overlooking six enormous columns soaring upward from where the Temple of Jupiter once stood. The total scenery was breathtaking.

The Acropolis of Baalbek is the largest and best preserved corpus of Roman architecture remaining in Lebanon. Baalbek became a Roman province of Syria, after Pompey conquered Ituraea, around A.D. 50. Many Ituraeans served in the Roman army and were famous for their horsemanship and their skill in archery. Philip the Tetrarch ruled Ituraea when the Word of God came to John the Baptist in the wilderness (Luke 3:1–2).

Naphish—Numerous

Naphish probably merged with the Hagarenes and went southward to the province of Hejer, near Saudi Arabia. Some Arabian historians contend that this tribe was known for hospitality and friendliness.

Kedemah—Toward the East

This tribe seems to have settled in eastern Arabia. The Hebrew word *kedem* means that which is immediately before or in front of something or someone. *Kuddam* is the

Arabic word for *kedem* and has the same meaning. Kedem is also used in a geographic connotation to describe a location or country immediately before or in front of another location or country in an easterly direction. For instance, when Abraham gave gifts to his six Arabian sons by Keturah, he sent them on their way "eastward . . . to the country of the east" (Gen. 25:6). Abraham was living in Canaan at that time, "and he directed his sons and their families toward the land lying immediately to the east of Palestine—Arabia and Mesopotamia (modern Iraq)."[15]

The Keturahites

All the Semitic Arabs and Jews are blood brothers, born of the same fathers, Eber and Abraham. Ishmael and the six sons of Keturah were Semitic through their father Abraham, and Hamitic through their mothers, Hagar and Keturah. After Sarah's death, "Abraham again took a wife, and her name was Keturah" (Gen. 25:1).

Zimran—Celebrated

The Arabian tribe Zimran has been traced to Zabram, a district of Ethiopia. Originally, the Sabeans migrated south and colonized Ethiopia, around the tenth century B.C., and the people settled near the Red Sea, west of Mecca. Some historians argue that Zimran may be identified with Beni Omran, whose descendants have not been clearly traced. *Beni* is the Arabic word for sons or descendants of a tribe.

Jokshan—Fowler

Jokshan settled on the borders of Palestine and his sons were Sheba and Dedan (Gen. 25:3). Their descendants were called the Sabaeans, or Dedanites. "The Sabaeans

The Keturahites

ABRAHAM AND KETURAH

ZIMRAN

JOKSHAN

MEDAN

MIDIAN

ISHBAK

SHUAH

were the most distinguished branch of the entire Arabian family. Seba, biblical Sheba, their original homeland, lay south of Najran in the Yaman district."[16] For more understanding about the Semitic Arabs, the reader is encouraged to consult Philip Hitti and the four volumes of William Smith (see Notes).

Medan—Judgment

Medan may have merged with Midian. The Midianites and the Ishmaelites were used of God to bring Joseph into "Egypt" (Gen. 37:36). The Medanites, Midianites, and Ishmaelites were related through intermarriage. Perhaps for this reason their names have been mentioned interchangeably in the Bible.

Midian—Place of Judgment

Midian is the progenitor of the Midianites. This tribe settled in the Arabian desert toward the southern part of the peninsula, along the eastern shore of the Gulf of Eyleh. The people also lived northward along the eastern borders of Palestine and toward the Sinai Peninsula, where Moses led the flock of Jethro, his father-in-law.

Ishbak—Leaving

Ishbak was the founder of a tribe living in northern Arabia in the valley of Sabak, located in Beni-Tameen, in Nejd, not far from the great desert of Yensu'ah and the sands of Yebreen, near the Persian Gulf.

Shuah—Prosperity

Some have incorrectly connected Shuah, the son of Abraham (Gen. 25:2) to Shuah, the father of Judah's Canaanite wife, "Shua" (Gen. 38:2, 12; cf. 1 Chron. 2:3). This Arabian tribe may have settled in the Persian Gulf, but it is hard to prove it because very little is known about this tribe.

So far we have seen a bird's-eye view concerning the origin and genealogy of the Semitic Arabs (see Gen. 10:26–29; 25:2, 13–15; 1 Chron. 1:20–23, 29–32). All the Arabian tribes can be traced to Joktan (Kahtan) and Abraham. The Arabs are Semitic and Hamitic. They are Semitic through Joktan and Abraham, and Hamitic through Hagar and Keturah. The Joktanites intermarried with the Canaanites, Assyrians, Cushites, Chaldaeans, and many other tribes. The Ishmaelites intermarried also with other tribes. In fact, the whole human race has gone through blood infusion by marrying across racial boundaries, and as a result, it is not possible to trace any pure human family.

These biblical and historical facts are seldom taught in Western schools and Bible colleges. It is amazing how these facts have been so generally overlooked by some biblical scholars and historians in the Western world. It seems to me that the deficiency displayed by these scholars as far as biblical and historical truths concerning the Arabs is remarkable indeed.

3

God's Encounter with Hagar

This unusual story must begin with a narrative of God's divine rendezvous with a castaway. The reason for this is that I marvel at God's miraculous intervention in the affairs of mankind and at His sovereignty in election. God calls out individuals from all walks of life to accomplish His good purposes in a variety of ways. He elects some for historic and prophetic roles, and others for eternal salvation. I believe that Hagar and her son, Ishmael, were undoubtedly chosen to fulfill their historical roles, and also to receive willingly God's gracious gift of everlasting life. After all, "the Son of Man has come to seek and to save that which was lost" (Luke 19:10).

The contrasting and controversial doctrines of divine sovereignty and human freedom have been plaguing biblical scholars for centuries and causing division and contention especially among Christians. Consequently, no attempt will be made to clarify these two distinct doctrines, mainly because no one is able to fathom "the depth of the riches both of the wisdom and knowledge of God! How unsearchable are His judgments and His ways past finding out!" (Rom.

11:33). The only sober way to explain what we cannot understand is to humbly agree with the Word of God.

God is perceived by many as whimsical and biased with lots of rules and no mercy. The drama of Hagar's predicament is a convincing illustration of God's mercy and compassion for the human race in general, and the disinherited and despised in particular. God is sovereign and only He can do what appears to be a foolish thing because "God has chosen the foolish things of the world to put to shame the wise . . . and the base things of the world and the things which are despised God has chosen . . . that no flesh should glory in His presence" (1 Cor. 1:27–29).

The story begins with an unprecedented appearance of God to a woman. In the quiet of the wilderness Hagar was confronted by the Angel of the Lord. It was an electrifying moment of indescribable significance, mainly because the Angel was not a created being—He was God manifesting Himself to Hagar. It was the first recorded visit of Jehovah to a woman. He had come to bring peace of mind and salvation to a disadvantaged and dejected young Egyptian bondmaid. It is of great importance to note that Hagar was the only woman in the Old Testament who spoke with God face-to-face for a long period of time.

The apostle John declares, "No one has seen God at any time" (John 1:18; cf. 1 John 4:12), because "God is Spirit" (John 4:24). Since God is Spirit and only He can be an adequate Counselor and Savior of mankind, God assumed visible human form in the Old Testament by veiling His glory in order to accomplish His sovereign plan of redemption by allowing a sinner to "live by his faith" (Hab. 2:4). The doctrine of justification by faith alone has been instituted by God in order to make the gift of salvation available to every person.

The appearances of God to His elected people are called "theophanies." According to my understanding of Scripture, when "the Angel of the Lord" or "the Angel of God" is mentioned in the Old Testament, the article "the" specifically denotes a pre-incarnate appearance of the Eternal Son of God, our Lord and Savior Jesus Christ.

What is so amazing and comforting about Hagar's narrative is that many of us can identify with her perplexing situation. Genesis 16 introduces Hagar as a clear indication of God's love and compassion for the despondent who obeys the voice of God. After being used and abused by Sarah, Hagar flees into the desert in total desperation. Suddenly, God appears to her with lengthy promises of great blessings for her and her posterity.

Most of us are not considered to be important in the world's eyes; we suffer and are unjustly treated as Hagar was. We may be at the end of our rope and feeling utterly rejected and abandoned. If so, the message of Genesis 16 ought to be personalized with the hope that we may emulate Hagar's obedient attitude. Remember this, God sees us and hears our affliction and cares for us. We are encouraged to cast "all your care upon Him, for He cares for you" (1 Peter 5:7).

Every time I try to visualize how Hagar must have felt the moment she realized that God was talking to her, my heart overflows with amazement and ecstasy. Since no one has talked with God face-to-face in the same manner Hagar did and under the same unique circumstances, and since no one was there to witness the lengthy interview by eavesdropping on the conversation, one has to have a great deal of imagination in order to be able to delineate what seemingly took place during that historic moment.

Imagination is a precious gift from God. It is the elixir of life which enables a person to see things that have always been there, but no one else could see them in the same descriptive way. Imagination gives man the ability to discover the beauty of that which has been hidden from the beginning of time. Imagination is a mental process consisting of creative perceptions. Because no one has been able to recapture the images of sights and sounds and moods of that historic moment of God's encounter with Hagar, I shall try to use my imagination to present a fair portrait of that unusual encounter, because imagination may also be helpful in establishing a mental conception of producing ideas consistent with reality.

Before expounding on Hagar's thrilling story which culminated with her lengthy interview with the Almighty, I would like to say that this unique account has been regretfully overlooked by most biblical scholars and others. As a result of such thoughtless and conditioned oversight, unevangelized Arabs and their counterparts have been robbed of discovering for themselves "the width and length and depth and height" of God's impartial love and mercy for the whole human race. Assuredly, God accepts every person who "fears Him and works righteousness" (Acts 10:35).

More often than not a reader may lose the main thought of the account if the setting of this exciting story is not explained in narrative form. Let us begin with Abraham.

Abraham was born around 2166 B.C. in Ur of the Chaldees. Idolatry and concubinage were practiced here. Abraham was conditioned by his heathen upbringing to practice idolatry and serve "other gods" (Josh. 24:2). Ur was located in the lower part of Mesopotamia, modern Iraq, not far from the head of the Persian Gulf. Ur was an important center of Sumerian culture. Sumer was located between the Tigris and Euphrates rivers, where they come together before spilling into the Arabian Gulf.

The name Sumer today designates the southern part of ancient Mesopotomia. Southern Mesopotamia was occupied at the time of Abraham by a people speaking a non-Semitic language with a different culture, known as Sumerians. Roughly 5,000 years ago, the Sumerians invented the cuneiform system of writing, which was done on mud tablets. Mud was also vital for building towns, cities, and temples. Modern Iraq still has a large brick factory at Nasiriyah. Not far from Nasiriyah, the monolithic bulk pyramid and the imposing ziggurat at Ur were built from mud bricks.

Mesopotamia was also inhabited by a people speaking Semitic languages. The mixture of the Sumerian and Semitic cultures produced, among other things, the Akkadian language, which was written with a cuneiform script.[1] The society of Abraham's day was very progressive and religious. "Artists were skilled, builders competent, business active, and times good. Religion centered in the worship of the moon-god Nanna."[2]

Abraham Leaves Ur

The times of Abraham were prosperous technologically and religiously, when God called him for a specific prophetic reason. Stephen tells us that Abraham was in Mesopotamia when God appeared to him and said, "Get out of your country and from your relatives, and come to a land that I will show you" (Acts 7:2–3).

At the time of the command, I believe Abraham was living in the same house with his father, Terah, his two brothers, Nahor and Haran, with Haran's two daughters, Milcah and Iscah, and Lot, Haran's son. Other relatives and servants also may have been living in or somewhere near that big house.

The reason for this is that God has initiated and instilled in the heart of man, presumably even before the time of Moses, to be accountable for the protection and welfare of one's parents and relatives. These inherent moral obligations made it very difficult for Abraham to leave Ur without his relatives. Later on, the inspired apostle Paul reiterated these same moral obligations in agreement with the Mosaic Law concerning the honoring, obeying, and revering of parents (see Eph. 6:1–3; cf. Ex. 20:12; Lev. 19:3).

I disagree with those who are postulating that Abraham disobeyed God by not leaving his relatives behind, as he was commanded to do. I dare say that God was only testing his faith and priorities, but not his action. God loves to test His servants in order that He may reward them according to "the thoughts and intents of [their] heart" (Heb. 4:12).

Conversely, God intervened in the life of Abraham, when he used human logic in order to protect his self-interest. On other occasions, Abraham pretended twice to be Sarah's brother in order to save his life, and also agreed with Sarah when she gave him Hagar "to be his wife," for the purpose of procreation (Gen. 12:17; 16:3; 20:18). Did God chasten Abraham and Sarah for their human contrivances? Of course not. Imagine if God punished us for every mistake we made. I believe God winks at many of our mistakes, mainly because "He remembers that we are dust" (Ps. 103:14). And also because He is so compassionate and merciful and does not act and think as we do. He said, "For My thoughts are not your thoughts, nor are your ways My ways. . . . For as the heavens are higher than the earth, so are My ways higher than your ways, and My thoughts than your thoughts" (Isa. 55:8–9). This should put to rest this argument.

It is interesting to note that this was and still is the custom in the Middle East. The younger generation is taught to obey, honor, and revere the older generation. Relatives usually live together under the same roof and interact with each other, somewhat similar to the days of Abraham. Each person feels a part of the family unit in which he or she is entitled to certain rights and committed to definite obligations. These privileges and duties are considered to be sacred and remain to this day a religious and moral principle. (I have neither heard nor seen a single Middle Easterner who had approved of sending away his parents or relatives to a convalescent home.)

After the untimely death of Haran at Ur, Abraham and Nahor took Sarai and Milcah as their wives. Sarai was ten years younger than Abraham. Josephus says that Iscah is another name for Sarai (Gen. 11:29), whose name was changed to Sarah, meaning "princess" (Gen. 17:15). Sarah was Abraham's half-sister; he himself says of her that she was the daughter of his father, but not the daughter of his mother (Gen. 20:12).

Marriages between relatives are common in the Middle East. These customs were inherited from the laws of the ancient world. It is believed that such marriages preserve the family's heritage and protect its financial inheritance from being usurped by strangers, or as I have heard some friends say, "Strangers may turn out to be charismatic swindlers." By taking Sarah as his own wife and adopting Lot as his son, Abraham not only had acted in accordance to the law of the land, but more importantly, he had proved to be responsible and trustworthy. His action underscores some of the many qualities which he would pass on to his posterity.

Abraham departed from his native country, with his father, Terah, his wife Sarah, his nephew Lot, and the rest of his family, and went to Haran. Haran was almost midway between Ur and Canaan, the Promised Land. Abraham's final destination was to travel "more than 1,000 miles in moving from Ur of the Chaldees to southern Canaan (Gen. 11:31—12:9)."[3] His first stopping place was Haran, some 600 miles northwest from Ur, and approximately 400 miles northeast from Canaan. Haran was situated in the southwestern district of Syria. "He went first to Haran because there were only two routes to the Promised Land available

at that time: across the Arabian desert, which was practically impossible, and along the Euphrates to Haran."[4]

Haran was located in Padan-Aram, meaning "the field or
plain of Aram." Aram founded Syria, and was the progenitor of the Aramaean people who gave us the Aramaic language. Aram was one of the five sons of Shem (Gen. 10:22).
The Aramaeans spread from Syria to Mesopotamia to
northern Palestine and beyond. Another name for Syria is
al-Sham in Arabic, meaning that it is derived from Shem.
The Arabs also called Damascus *al-Sham*.

It appears that the cities of Haran, Syria, and Nahor, Mesopotamia, were named after Abraham's two brothers. The
wives of Isaac and Jacob were fetched from these two cities
(Gen. 24:10; 28:2, 5). Jacob spent fourteen years in the region of Haran until all his children were born there.

Like Ur, Haran was a commercial city and a natural stopping place for Abraham and his clan. It was the caravan
route connecting Damascus, Nineveh, and other cities in
Mesopotamia, Palestine, and Egypt. It was also a center of
idolatry. The people worshiped the moon-god, Sin.

Parenthetically, the chosen people of God, whether they
may be Jews or Gentiles, have always been surrounded and
afflicted by evil practices and temptations. This truth has
been amplified by our Lord Jesus in the parable of the
wheat and tares (Matt. 13:24–30). In my opinion, the evil
which epitomizes all evils is prominent in man's inhumanity
to man. Fortunately, the day will come when the kingdom of
God shall invade the stream of history and destroy the vi-
cious cycles of all evil practices.

Aramaic was adopted as the *lingua franca* for the leading
nations of ancient times, including Assyria and Babylonia.
Some portions of Daniel and Ezra were originally written in
Aramaic, the same language which was spoken by the Jews
at the time of Christ. Jesus cried out from the cross in Ara-

maic, saying, "Eloi, Eloi, lama sabachthani?" which is translated, "My God, My God, why have You forsaken Me?" (Matt. 27:46; Mark 15:34). It could also be translated in the vernacular, "But for this purpose I came to this hour" (John 12:27). Apparently, the children of Aram had more interaction with the descendants of Abraham than the rest of the peoples in the early days, and were influenced by much of their life-style.

Abraham Leaves Haran

No one really knows how long Abraham stayed in Haran. It seems that he was utterly content to remain there for a long, long time, because his father was growing older and weaker and was not able to travel again. Abraham was surrounded by relatives and friends who may have influenced his decision. I surmise that his wife had the greatest influence by persuading him to stay in that lively and friendly place. Seeing that he had no urgent reason to go through the hardship of moving his family again, and this time to a land that he knew not, he decided to defer his journey to Canaan for a more convenient time.

Conversely, God had more important plans for Abraham. He chose him so that He would be able to use him as a vessel in order to fulfill His divine plans. When "Terah died in Haran" (Gen. 11:32), God removed Abraham from that city, and led him into the land of promise. Among other important things, Canaan was designed not only to try his faith and obedience, but also to separate him from the world and set him apart for special services. This has been God's method in dealing with those whom He chooses to set apart for Himself. They must go through seminary training in Canaan before He can use them effectively. Many are serving God for selfish motives without having lived in Canaan.

"So Abram departed as the Lord had spoken to him. . . .

And Abram was seventy-five years old when he departed from Haran" (Gen. 12:4). He took his wife, his nephew, "and all their possessions that they had gathered, and the people |servants| whom they had acquired in Haran, and. . . . came to the land of Canaan" (Gen. 12:5).

Canaan was approximately 400 miles southwest of Haran. It was a long journey for them on camels and donkeys. After several days of travel, they arrived at Shechem, which was located in the center of Canaan between Mount Ebal and Mount Gerizim. God was leading him step-by-step because he knew not "where he was going" (Heb. 11:8).

After a short time, Abraham moved on to Bethel, twenty miles south of Shechem and about ten miles north of Jerusalem. Abraham must have liked Bethel because that is where he settled until he separated from Lot, after he returned from Egypt with Hagar.

Abraham "built an altar to the Lord" in Shechem and Bethel (Gen. 12:7–8). He did that after God appeared to him again, not only to acknowledge his Lord and Savior publicly, but also to publish his faith to all those peoples among whom he had come to live. Having become an exemplary witness of his faith and obedience, Abraham "was called the friend of God" (James 2:23). Obedience is a prerequisite for such an exclusive privilege. The Lord Jesus concurs with this truth by saying, "You are My friends if you do whatever I command you" (John 15:14).

It is imperative to point out at this time that Abraham was not saved from eternal hell in a tent meeting, or in a Billy Graham crusade, but God Himself "preached the gospel to Abraham beforehand" (Gal. 3:8). To this day I have never heard a sermon preached on this most exciting topic. I believe that God preached the gospel of salvation to Abraham during His first appearance to him in Mesopotamia (Acts 7:2). God brought him to Himself by an effectual call and snatched him as a branch out of the fire. Abraham was fully persuaded by the irresistible power of God's grace, which is freely offered to every person by the unmerited favor and love of God.

I am utterly convinced that Abraham's saving faith came "by hearing, and hearing by the word of God" (Rom. 10:17). Abraham must have heard the gospel from the mouth of "the Christ, the Savior of the world" (John 4:42). The Lord Jesus declared to the unconverted Jews of His day that He is the "I AM" (JEHOVAH GOD); and that Abraham rejoiced to see His day, "and he saw it and was glad" (John 8:56–58)! Genuine "salvation can be received only by grace through faith, and faith involves knowledge of the gospel of Christ, and knowledge includes acceptance of and adherence to the truth of the gospel."[5]

Abraham in Egypt

The first severe trial of Abraham's faith came when God sent a grievous famine to "the land" (Gen. 12:10). Abraham and his people had never been accustomed to such hardship, and their faith was not yet tested. I can visualize the complaining of his wife and spoiled nephew, and also the murmuring of his people. Some of them probably murmured against Abraham as the Israelites did against Moses. We should know that trials are designed to help us learn to trust God, not only when our needs are met, but also when suffering and privation come our way. Suffering is still a mystery to me. Suffering should bring us to the foot of the cross in order for us to learn about this mystery and be able to overcome it. Sometimes it pleases God to try with great afflictions those whom He chooses for special services, in order to strengthen their faith and reliance on Him alone.

When Abraham saw that the land could no longer sustain his people and flocks, he made a wise decision by exercising his God-given common sense and journeyed on south toward Egypt. His prudence made use of the opportunity to sojourn there until the famine was over. Since Sarah was a beautiful woman, Abraham feared that her beauty would tempt the Egyptians and put his life in danger. So he persuaded her to pass for his sister. This term is used in Hebrew, as in many other languages, to designate a niece, and this is exactly what she was.

Egypt is called by the Arabs *Misr*. The Canaanites called it *Mizri*, a derivation from Mizraim, who founded Egypt soon after the Flood. The Pyramids and great Sphinx were built before the time of Abraham. The Amarna Tablets and the Pyramid Texts show a high degree of civilization in Egypt and its strong, centralized government. I am sure that Abraham witnessed these historical facts, and his trip to the land of the Pharaohs proved to be providential.

It was a common practice in early times for men of power to seize beautiful women. (See King David and Bathsheba in 2 Sam. 11.) Abraham was well aware of the Pharaoh's reputation, and he did precisely what any man of tradition would do. He asked his wife to pass for his sister, hoping that the Pharaoh would spare his life and leave them alone. Sarah obeyed her husband. What transpired after that is most exciting.

The scene opens with Sarah waiting in a big house to meet the Pharaoh, meaning "great house." I cannot imagine how Sarah reacted when she was "commended" by the princes of Pharaoh as a prime candidate to become one of his harem (Gen. 12:15). I presume that she reasoned with herself and believed that God led her there for His good purpose and that He would protect her and her husband from all harm. She had already witnessed God's dealings with Abraham and his family, and she had no reason to doubt now.

Sarah was very beautiful, but her real beauty was from within. I think she would have done any reasonable thing that her husband had asked her to do for his welfare. She was an exemplary person, and all God-fearing women are encouraged to emulate her. Her duty as a wife was to be in subjection to her godly husband, whom she honored and called "my lord" (Gen. 18:12). This does not mean that she was inferior to her husband. On the contrary, both respected and honored each other. Abraham was a blessed man for having a wife whose inner beauty was "very precious in the sight of God. For in this manner, in former times, the holy women who trusted in God also adorned themselves, being submissive to their own husbands, as Sarah obeyed Abraham, calling him lord" (1 Peter 3:4–6).

Let us not forget that God is sovereign and nothing can happen without His foreknowledge and His permission. Let us also remember that Abraham and Sarah were chosen to be the progenitors of Arabs and Jews. More important than that, they were chosen so that the "Seed" of Abraham, "who is Christ," should "come to seek and to save that which was lost" (Gal. 3:16; cf. Luke 19:10). For this reason, I believe that God led Sarah to the house of Pharaoh and would not allow him to take her as his "wife" (Gen. 12:19).

While Sarah was treated with great admiration at the Pharaoh's entourage and getting acquainted with his large family, Abraham was lavished with presents for her sake. Outwardly, both of them were able to play the game and hide their true love for each other and act contented. No doubt they were miserable from the moment the princes of Pharaoh confiscated Sarah, and were driven to much prayer during many sleepless nights.

The seeming reality of losing his wife was unbearable to Abraham. I expect that he fell on his face many times and cried out to God for help with a remorseful heart. Humans make mistakes, and often their grasp of logic could entirely lead them to trouble. But Abraham "was called the friend of God" (James 2:23), and when he called upon God with fervent cries of repentance, the heart of God was kindled, and "the Lord plagued Pharaoh and his house with great plagues because of Sarai, Abram's wife" (Gen. 12:17).

We are not told what these plagues were, but they were sufficient to convince the terrified Pharaoh, and his princes who had commended Sarah to him, that these plagues were for Sarah's sake. The Pharaoh may have been alarmed by the plagues and understood that Abraham and his wife were special favorites of heaven. God's people sin like anyone else, and when they sin they are chastised according to the gravity of their sin. "My son, do not despise the chastening of the Lord, Nor be discouraged when you are rebuked by Him. For whom the Lord loves He chastens, And scourges every son whom He receives" (Heb. 12:5–6). Abraham and Sarah made many mistakes in their lives, but God turned many of them into a blessing. We are reminded "that all things work together for good to those who love God, to those who are the called according to His purpose" (Rom. 8:28).

Subsequently, the Pharaoh gave Abraham additional gifts in order to appease "the wrath of Heaven." He gave him more donkeys, camels, sheep, servants, gold, and silver. "Abram was very rich in livestock, in silver, and in gold" (Gen. 13:2). Nonetheless, the greatest gift was given to Sarah. According to the Midrash, a collection of an early Jewish commentary on biblical texts, the Pharaoh gave his young daughter to Sarah when he witnessed the miracles brought upon him by the plagues. He is reported saying, "It is better for Hagar to be a slave in Sarah's house than mistress in her own."[6]

In this sense Hagar's name is interpreted as reward ("Ha-Agar, this is reward"). Another explanation of "Ha-Agar" is "to adorn." It has been said that she was adorned with beauty and piety and good deeds. Also, the Soncino Chumash, a Jewish commentary of Old Testament texts, supports the Midrash concerning Hagar being the Pharaoh's daughter. The moment Hagar met Sarah she befriended her, and when she saw the miracles which were wrought on Sarah's behalf, she said, "I will rather be a servant in her house than mistress in my own."[7] Many commentaries and reliable biblicists believe that Hagar is the daughter of the Pharaoh. I am mentioning only a few of them in this chapter.

In the enumeration of the ten trials of Abraham by Pirke de Rabbi Eliezer we read:

> R. Joshua ben Korchah said: Because of his love for her [Sarah], [Pharaoh] wrote in her marriage document [giving her] all his wealth, whether in silver or in gold, or in manservants, or land, and he wrote [giving her] the land of Goshen for a possession. Therefore the children of Israel dwelt in the land of Goshen, in the land of their mother Sarah. He [also] wrote [giving] her Hagar, his daughter from a concubine, as her handmaid. And whence do we know that Hagar was the daughter of Pharaoh? Because it is said, "Now Sarai Abraham's wife bare him no children; and she had an handmaid, an Egyptian, whose name was Hagar" (Gen. 16:1).[8]

Pirke de Rabbi Eliezer also quotes another version of the tradition that Hagar was the daughter of the Pharaoh found in Genesis, Midrash Rabbah 45:1:

> And she had a handmaid whose name was Hagar. She had a handmaid of usufruct (Abraham could use her dowry without any accountability) and he was bound to support her and was not permitted to sell her. R. Simeon b. Yohai said: Hagar was the daughter of Pharaoh. When Pharaoh saw what had been done to Sarah in his house he took his daughter and gave her to him [Abraham] saying, "It is better that my daughter be a handmaid in this house than the mistress of another." Thus it is written "And she had a handmaid named Hagar," he saying "Here is your reward (agar)."[9]

The same tradition is also preserved in the Palestinian *Targum*. In rabbinic tradition, Hagar was not merely the handmaid of Sarah; she was considered to be royalty, the daughter of Pharaoh, given as a servant to Sarah by her father.

As I have said previously, nothing can take God by surprise. He is infinite in power and possesses infinite knowledge and wisdom. God foreknew that Hagar would play an important role in the dispensation of the Abrahamic Covenant in relation to his physical seed; and that she would become the ancestress of "a great nation" (Gen. 21:18).

Long before the birth of Ishmael, I believe Hagar was chosen as a vessel for the purpose of procreation. Now I can understand the reason why the Lord restrained Sarah "from bearing children" (Gen. 16:2), until He fulfilled His redemptive plan concerning Hagar and Ishmael. God loves the human race and desires that people from all walks of life should come to "know Him and the power of His resurrection" (Phil. 3:10). Another reason for restraining Sarah from childbearing was because God wanted to demonstrate His miraculous power. God said, "Is anything too hard for the Lord?" (Gen. 18:14).

What is so unique about this believable tradition is how Hagar condescended to become a slave. It is comforting for us who believe in the sovereignty of God to know with assurance that nothing can happen by accident, and to realize that the actions of man have never taken God by surprise. God is in total control of His creation, and He always works things out for His good purpose. As far as Hagar's destiny is concerned, God had predetermined in His foreknowledge to make Abraham's journey to Egypt successful and providential, and to fulfill His sovereign plan for the human race to "be fruitful and multiply; fill the earth" (Gen. 1:28; cf. 9:1, 7; 16:10; 17:20). So Abraham was sent "away, with his wife and all that he had" (Gen. 12:20).

Abraham Returns to Canaan

All that I have written so far is a prelude to the forthcoming account of God's meeting with Hagar in the wilderness. With this in mind, let's move from Egypt to Canaan, where the marriage between Abraham and Hagar was consummated for the purpose of procreation. Sarah deduced from presumptive evidence that God may not give her children at her old age of seventy-five. She said to Abraham, "See now, the Lord has restrained me from bearing children. Please, go in to my maid; perhaps I shall obtain children by her" (Gen. 16:2).

Many put the blame on Sarah for inducing her husband to betroth Hagar and for approving of their contractual marriage. They also criticize Abraham for agreeing with his wife's plan to use Hagar. It is a common behavioral pattern for people to act as judicators in relation to other people, particularly when they themselves are not involved with a similar circumstance.

I heard recently a famous televangelist preach on this very topic, saying, "If not for Abraham's sin of adultery with Hagar, we would not have had the Arabs with us today." This statement betrays a wounded spirit and a prejudiced heart. Similar harsh and unkind utterances about the Arabs have been for some time promulgated by many televangelists and their counterparts in order to promote the nation of Israel. Scriptural references relating to Arabs have been blown out of proportion and woven into the very fabric of Western political theology. It seems that the more uncertain these people are about the true nature and character of God, the more earnestly they try to parrot their "particular hermeneutical methods based upon their own cultural and ethnic conditioning."[10]

I have rarely heard a sermon criticizing Jacob for sleeping with Bilhah and Zilpah, the handmaids of his two wives,

Leah and Rachel. Four out of the twelve sons of Jacob were born from the two servants. In any case, Abraham and Jacob acted in concert with the historical custom of their day. This practice took place long before the Mosaic Law.

The Nuzi Tablets gave us much information about Abraham's day concerning early customs and practices. Nuzi was an ancient city located near southern Khurdistan, and some 150 miles north of Baghdad, Iraq. The American School of Oriental Research and Harvard University excavated Nuzi in 1925 through 1931.

According to these tablets, a trusted servant could be adopted as a legal heir to his foster parent's property. But if a natural son was born, he would become the rightful heir. Abraham adopted Eliezer as his legal heir, because Abraham and Sarah were childless (Gen. 15:2). If a wife was barren, she was allowed to furnish her husband with a girl servant as a secondary wife, but the first wife was entitled to claim the newborn son as her own. Marriage was considered mainly for bearing children and not for companionship. If the secondary wife should have a son, the law required that the son should not be expelled and disinherited. Only a divine intervention could overrule this human law.

Another custom illuminated is that found in Genesis 12:10–20; 20:2–6; 26:1–11, where the wife of a patriarch is introduced as his sister with no apparent worthy reason. The texts from Nuzi, however, show that among the Hurrians marriage bonds were most solemn, and the wife had legally, although not necessarily through ties of blood, the simultaneous status of sister, so that the term "sister" and "wife" could be interchangeable in an official use under certain circumstances. Thus, in resorting to the wife-sister relationship, both Abraham and Isaac were availing themselves of the strongest safeguards the law, as it existed then, could afford them.[11]

Abraham and Isaac did not lie willfully, as modern Bible scholars suppose, when they passed their wives as their sisters. They were simply trying to protect their self-interests in accordance with the customs of their time.

Abraham had possibly more than a thousand servants, counting the young and the old. He acquired them from Ur, Haran, Egypt and Canaan. Hundreds of them "were born in his own house" (Gen. 14:14). His most trusted servant was Eliezer, "who ruled over all that he had" (Gen. 24:2). Sarah's favorite servant was Hagar.

If Hagar was really the Pharaoh's daughter, as several commentaries have suggested, and as evidenced by the foregoing, the credibility of the story becomes more intriguing. Only God can create the circumstances by which the three characters of Genesis 16, namely Abraham and Sarah and Hagar, would meet in Canaan under the same tent, and collaborate in order to fulfill God's predestined plan for them and their posterity. This hypothesis may offend some conservative theologians, but please be patient until you discover with me how gracious and compassionate God is, and how He turned the seemingly bad experience of these three characters into great blessings for all concerned.

God Appears to Hagar

Hagar seems to have occupied a prominent place in Abraham's life and brought him not only a physical seed and other rewards, but also an inward spiritual participation in the faith of his God. She was probably added to the family of faith during Abraham's sojourn in Egypt.

This should bring us to the thrilling episode of Hagar's encounter with her Savior. I believe Hagar's salvation was confirmed when God visited her, mainly because He is not in the habit of appearing to individuals "whose names have not been written in the Book of Life of the Lamb slain from the foundation of the world" (Rev. 13:8; 17:8). This is the most exciting scene in the whole story. No one can really describe the ambiance of that particular moment, when God Himself came to Hagar in "the wilderness" to "speak comfort to her" (Hos. 2:14). When she was driven forth into the wilderness by the jealous harshness of Sarah, "the Angel of the Lord found her by a spring of water in the wilderness, by the spring on the way to Shur" (Gen. 16:7).

Shur was an area between Beer-Sheba and Egypt and probably was an uninhabited caravan route suitable for pasturing flocks. On her way from Egypt to Canaan, Hagar traveled through the wilderness of the Negev and Sinai. She knew that area very well, when "the pregnant Hagar had sought refuge in it from the burning wrath of her barren mistress, Sarai."[12]

The well was called Be'er-la-hai-ro'i (the Well-of-the-Living-One-Who-Seeth). It is located "between Kadesh and Bered" (Gen. 16:14). The exact location of Bered is uncertain, but that of Kadesh is known. Kadesh is identified with the fertile gardens of Wadi-el-Qudeirat in Sinai and watered by the spring of Ain-el-Qudeirat. It is possible that Hagar met God there. Also, this is where "the wilderness of Paran" is located. Ishmael and his people dwelt in that region (Gen. 21:21). Hagar and her kin were deeply rooted in Sinai, with which her name became synonymous (Gal. 4:22–25).

When Hagar reached Shur, meaning "wall" or "fortification," she rested from her long journey before crossing the border. The Egyptians had built a strong line of forts there for protection against invaders from the east. This information is mentioned in ancient Egyptian records dating back as early as 2,000 B.C. This is where Hagar was confronted by the Angel of the Lord, who had come to bring her comfort and eternal security.

That was a moment of paramount significance, mainly because the Angel of the Lord was not a created being, but He was Jehovah manifesting Himself to Hagar. It is evident from the conversation that He spoke and acted as God with full authority. His appearance to Hagar is the first recorded visit of God to the earth.[13]

In attempting to write about the Lord's adorable Person and His incomprehensible ways, my finite mind is unable to describe adequately the scene under discussion. Human pens falter when trying to delineate the degree of Hagar's exhilaration the moment she realized that she was in the presence of the Almighty. Unfortunately, I have tried in vain to find materials written on this topic from a positive approach. Many authors have perceived Hagar as an arrogant and disobedient slave, and they were conditioned to believe that God did "cast out the bondwoman and her son" (Gal. 4:30). I will try to explain this later on.

Let us now visualize how God treated Hagar's predicament. The scene opens with Hagar lying down on the ground under the thin shadow of a palm tree, not far from the "spring of water in the wilderness" (Gen. 16:7). As far as her eyes could see there was nothing but drifting sand which was humped like the waves of a petrified sea. Beyond the palm tree, she saw a dust trail leading to Egypt, her beloved country. She looked above and saw the beautiful blue skies overlooking the desert expanse. Not a sound, not even a breath of life or so it seemed, when suddenly, she heard a voice calling her tenderly, "Hagar, Sarai's maid, where have you come from, and where are you going?" (Gen. 16:8).

We note here that God did not meet Hagar's desperate need until He brought her into the wilderness. Rightly considered, all the characters whom God chose for specific services had to be brought into the wilderness. This is where He met them and gave them their respective calling. These men and women became spiritual giants only because of

God's special work in their lives. This does not mean that the work of God is restricted to the mighty alone. Each person who really has no stature in the world's terms is also the clear object of God's love and provision and is called to play a special role in life. Hagar was called to be both a slave and the ancestress of "a great nation" (Gen. 21:18). She was a type of Christ, who condescended to become a servant. The Old Testament is replete with typology. It is astonishing to realize how God can take people from all walks of life and use them to accomplish His good purposes.

The Lord started the conversation by calling her Hagar, meaning to emigrate. It is reassuring to know that God "calls his own sheep by name" (John 10:3). He knew all about her problems, but He wanted to give her the opportunity to air her grief by way of a confession, so He could cleanse her soul from all obstructive feelings toward her mistress, Sarah. Confession of sins is required before God can fulfill His sovereign plan in and through the lives of His servants (1 John 1:9).

He asked her a leading question, "Where have you come from, and where are you going?" This is a beautiful way to start a conversation with people, especially if they need direction, peace of mind, and hope. This kind of approach will never fail to accomplish positive results, because "love will cover a multitude of sins" (1 Peter 4:8).

Hagar responded by saying, "I am fleeing from the presence of my mistress Sarai" (Gen. 16:8). No doubt while the Lord was listening to her despondency patiently and compassionately, Hagar's heart was immediately regenerated by His loving gazes at her weary countenance.

After she recounted her story in minute detail and was cleansed from all hindrances and ready to be used as a willing vessel, the Lord commanded her by saying, "Return to your mistress, and submit yourself under her hand" (Gen. 16:9).

I could not understand at first why the Lord commanded Hagar to go back and live under such grueling circumstances. After much reflection I concluded that she was sent back for good reasons. God wanted to use her as a witness of His ineffable love which compelled her to total submission and obedience to His irresistible, sovereign will, and to tell about His soothing words which enveloped her "as a hen gathers her chicks under her wings" (Matt. 23:37) and brought complete healing to her aching heart. Submission to God's authority provides providential protection and many blessings. Hagar's story is a good example of this truth.

Similarly, the Lord went from Jerusalem to Jacob's well in Sychar (near modern Nablus) in order to keep His foreordained rendezvous with a Samaritan woman. After her conversion, she "went her way into the city, and said to the men. . . . And many of the Samaritans of that city believed in Him because of the word of the woman" (John 4:28–39). Certainly these two extraordinary women ought to be emulated especially by "lukewarm" Christians (Rev. 3:16). The two women met God at a well. The well is a type of the Holy Spirit, who is like "a fountain of water springing up into everlasting life" (John 4:14).

Another good reason for the command was to provide a godly home for Ishmael, where he could be trained "in the way he should go, And when he is old he will not depart from it" (Prov. 22:6). This prescription was fulfilled when Abraham realized that Ishmael was a gift from God, who belonged exclusively to Him. Ishmael was reared in a godly home and was taught to do what God wanted him to do. His father and mother were good examples of this kind of behavior.

More than that, God was planning to make of Abraham a multitude of nations, and also to make Ishmael "a great nation" (Gen. 17:20). But first, Ishmael had to learn with the passing of years the apprenticeship of leadership and its obligations.

After her lengthy interview with the Lord, Hagar returned quickly to her mistress with a regenerated heart and a submissive attitude. She could hardly wait to reach the tent so she could share what the Lord promised her concerning Ishmael.

4

Ishmael, Prince of the Desert

Hagar's dilemma with her mistress' natural desire to use her as a surrogate mother has been interpreted deductively by many Christians and others. They contend that Hagar became arrogant, insolent, insubordinate, and hateful toward her mistress "when [Hagar] saw that she had conceived" (Gen. 16:4).

I believe Hagar did not hate her mistress personally—as a multitude of commentators surmise—she actually hated Sarah's stubborn determination to claim possession of the unborn child. The reason for Hagar's strong feelings of disgust with and objection to Sarah's selfish scheme is because God has instilled in the mind of a normal mother an instinct to love and nurture her own baby. God was planning to give each of them her own son and to bless them accordingly.

Apparently when Hagar told her mistress that she would not and could not give up her child, Sarah's dreams were shattered and abruptly she became hysterical. This is when she seems to have lost control, and with her husband's acquiescence, she afflicted her servant with bodily punishment. Passionate jealousy and bitterness set the two women against each other, and their relationship grew from bad to worse. Hagar could no longer live under existing circumstances; she decided to run away "from her presence" (Gen. 16:6).

Barrenness was and still is viewed with contempt and disgrace in the Middle East. Sterile wives were usually replaced by fertile women. This may seem a cruel treatment of wives who were unable to procreate, but really it was not. The custom allowed a barren wife to give her maid to her husband for the purpose of procreation. It was common for the latter woman to become the husband's favorite if she bore him a son. That was the scenario of Hagar's drama when her mistress became jealous and mistreated her.

In essence, after she came back from her unusual wilderness experience, Hagar may have said to her mistress something like this: "I empathize with your sterile condition and your legitimate desire to help my master obtain an heir by proxy through me. Forgive me for refusing to submit to your desire, and what 'you meant evil against me . . . God meant it for good'" (Gen. 50:20). Undoubtedly, from that time the ambivalent relationship of the two women was healed from the bitter feelings caused beforehand.

Now the scene opens with Abraham and Sarah sitting on a goatskin rug inside the tent, listening attentively to Hagar's tale of her confrontation with the God of Abraham. When she finished telling about her interview with God and His promises to her, Abraham rejoiced, believing that Hagar's son would be the promised heir (Gen. 15:4).

The Lord knew Hagar's thoughts and the intents of her heart very well. He knew that Hagar did the right thing when she refused to submit to her mistress's unscrupulous deal. No one is able to hide anything from God, because "all things are naked and open to the eyes of Him to whom we must give account" (Heb. 4:13). Hagar had sown in tears of affliction, and now she would reap joyfully. Her exemplary submissive attitude to God's sovereignty resulted in the forthcoming harvest of blessings. "Then the Angel of the Lord said to her, 'I will multiply your descendants exceedingly, so that they shall not be counted for multitude'" (Gen. 16:10).

Hagar was honest and transparent. She listened to the Lord's voice and yielded her whole being to Him with complete obedience. She followed His direction without compromise. Many people claim to be submissive to God's absolute authority, but their conditioned life-style reveals the opposite. Hagar is a good example of total submission to God's will. In Arabic, the word *Islam* means "submission," that is, submission to the will of God.

Submission to God's will should lead to humility, and humility should lead to faith in God, and faith in God provides His unmerited favor and love to those who have faith like Hagar's. God plucked out the root of pride from the innermost part of her soul and gave her grace so He could use her as a clean vessel, because "God resists the proud, But gives grace to the humble" (James 4:6). Grace could be defined as the desire and strength God gives to the humble to do His will.

However, how could anyone submit to an unknown and impersonal god? The Bible declares that it is only through the Lord and Savior Jesus Christ that it is at all possible to know God in a personal way. The same God with whom Hagar spoke face-to-face, "He has appointed a day on which He will judge the world in righteousness by the Man [Jesus Christ] whom he has ordained. He has given assurance of this to all by raising Him from the dead" (Acts 17:31).

Hagar heard Abraham and Sarah telling her about the Lord, but now she saw Him and spoke to Him for a long time. No one can remain the same after such a unique experience. Subsequently, Hagar presented herself for service as "a living sacrifice, holy, acceptable to God" (Rom. 12:1). The fulfillment of the first promise will be explored in the next chapter.

Soon after the first promise was given, the Lord said to Hagar: "Behold, you are with child, And you shall bear a son. *You shall call his name Ishmael,* Because the Lord has heard your affliction" (Gen. 16:11, emphasis added).

This is the first recorded instance where we read that the Almighty is a hearing God. It is so comforting to know that God's heart moves with compassion when He hears the bitter cries of the afflicted. Just as He came to the rescue of Adam and Eve when they had sinned, so also He comes now "to seek and to save" Hagar (Luke 19:10). There is a parallel in both of these stories. The parallel teaches us that God is much more interested in us than we can ever be interested either in Him or in our own welfare.

Paul declares that "there is none who seeks after God" (Rom. 3:11). Hagar was not seeking after God. She was running away from everyone, but God sought her and brought her to Himself, and gave her "the Spirit of adoption" (Rom. 8:15). From that moment on, she was set free from bondage and became the slave of God.

The Lord's heartening words eradicated Hagar's heavy burden and gave her "rest" (Matt. 11:28). It is a great solace to a woman with child to know that she is under God's care. God assured Hagar that she would bear a son, which Abraham desired, and she should call his name Ishmael, meaning God hears.

We come now to a most abused and misconstrued prediction concerning Ishmael's character and temperament. The Lord said, "He shall be a wild man; His hand shall be against every man, And every man's hand against him. And he shall dwell in the presence of all his brethren" (Gen. 16:12). All the things God said to Hagar were in the positive. He came to her in love and compassion and not in judgment. Although He was addressing Hagar with comforting words,

His words ought to be taken seriously by us because, "For whatever things were written before were written for our learning, that we through the patience and comfort of the Scriptures might have hope" (Rom. 15:4; cf. 1 Cor. 10:11). Hagar is a good example of God's unspeakable love for the human race.

The great majority of Western biblical scholars and others have been unknowingly mortifying and vilifying the Arab world by appealing to Genesis 16:12. Hardly a day goes by in the West when someone is not proclaiming that Ishmael was created "a wild ass of a man," and that his descendants have inherited his animalistic character and temperament. This kind of characterization benefits no one. It only reinforces prejudice and ignorance concerning the Arabs and obscures the fact that God wanted Ishmael to become "a great nation" (Gen. 17:20; cf. 21:18).

When the Lord said that Ishmael "shall be a wild man," I believe that He intended to prepare Ishmael to withstand the hardships of desert life. Remember that God promised five blessings to Hagar, and not one of them is in the negative. God wanted Ishmael to become prince of the desert, strong and insensitive to the extremity of desert climate, extravagant, gregarious, spirited, hardy with a boundless love of freedom as he rides on his camel or horse, revelling in the varied beauty of nature. These distinguishing characteristics have been passed on to his descendants.

God did not say that Ishmael would be "a wild ass of a man," the commentators who translated the word *wild man* said that. This description of Ishmael connotes a revolutionary and fugitive characterization of him and his descendants. And by doing so, commentators have succeeded in convincing the public that the Arabs are exactly what God made them to be—"barbarians."

The Hebrew word translated as wild ass is *pere*. Historically this word denoted one who was free-spirited and unrestrained. *Pere* was not used to mean savage or untamed as it is commonly understood in modern times.

Ishmael was created, like any other person, in God's image and according to His likeness (Gen. 1:26). However, Ishmael was a type of "the flesh" (Gal. 4:23). A symbol, or type, is a historical fact that symbolizes a spiritual truth. (I shall develop this theme when we reach the casting out of Hagar and her son from Abraham's household [Gal. 4:30].)

"His hand shall be against every man, and every man's hand against him. And he shall dwell in the presence of all his brethren" (Gen. 16:12). This promise emphasizes the unshackled and unrestrained desert life of Ishmael and his descendants. History attests to the fact that no nation was able to subjugate the Arabs by coercion or to uproot them from their biblical habitat. Ishmael lived and "died in the presence of all his brethren" (Gen. 25:18). The best way to deal with the man of "the flesh" is to imitate God's dealing with Hagar.

"Then she called the name of the Lord who spoke to her, ['El Roi'] You-Are the-God-Who-Sees" (Gen. 16:13). Hagar was overjoyed and enthralled by the realization that she had been in the very presence of Almighty God, without fear and trembling. She declared in the same verse, "Have I also here seen Him who sees me?" It is beyond anyone's capability to describe the exact feelings of Hagar at that particular moment. I have been calling her by her proper name, mainly because God called her Hagar (Gen. 16:8). Not only did God call her by name and speak to her, but she also saw Him and spoke to Him face-to-face. This should prove the belief that Jehovah Himself appeared to Hagar.

Ishmael's Upbringing

"So Hagar bore Abram a son; and Abram named his son, whom Hagar bore, Ishmael" (Gen. 16:15).

Abraham was anticipating the birth of his son with great expectation because Hagar had told him everything the Lord had said to her. We know this because God commanded her to "call his name Ishmael" and she did not, but Abraham did. Abraham was eighty-six years old when his son was born (Gen. 16:16). Ishmael was the first person to be given a name by God Himself. Abraham believed that Ishmael was indeed the promised seed who would become the heir of his house (Gen. 15:4).

Imagine how Abraham must have felt when he first heard the cries of the newborn babe, and how proud he was to become a father. The news flashed as lightning throughout the region, announcing the birth of Ishmael. Abraham's servants celebrated with singing and dancing, and Abraham made a great feast according to the customs of his day. Several lambs were slaughtered and roasted whole, and everyone present was treated lavishly. Abraham's passion and obsession for hospitality and generosity were passed on to Ishmael and his descendants.

During the first thirteen years of Ishmael's upbringing, his parents taught him to fear and obey the Lord. His father trained him in courage, hospitality, honesty, generosity, courtesy, and loyalty. Most likely he pampered him and gave him every whim and wish.

Ishmael grew up in the perfect, free atmosphere of the desert. He befriended the hardy nomads who tended his father's flocks and who looked up to him with mingled feelings of pride and affection as the son and heir of their master Abraham. Ishmael became known as chivalrous and established himself as the prince of the hardy nomads who served his father, and now they would also serve him. Abraham himself had apparently groomed his son for leadership and encouraged his servants to honor him.

Ishmael blossomed out into a true prince of the desert and was accustomed from childhood not only to luxury and extravagance, but also to the rugged desert life as evidenced by the feuds which raged often between his father's servants and the roving bands of free looters (Gen. 14:14). These events served to shape Ishmael's coveted life-style.

Unexpected Shock

God appeared again to Abraham when he "was ninety-nine years old" (Gen. 17:1). Thirteen years had gone by since Ishmael's birth. He was born at Mamre, near Hebron in Canaan, where Abraham's dwelling place was located (Gen. 18:1; cf. 23:19). Abraham was evidently strongly attached to his first and only son so far, and seems to have regarded him as the sole heir to his house.

Just as everything was going well for Abraham and Ishmael, God appeared to Abraham, saying, "Sarah your wife shall bear you a son, and you shall call his name Isaac; I will establish My covenant with him for an everlasting covenant, and with his descendants after him" (Gen. 17:19; cf. Gal. 3:29). This is the first time the name of Isaac is mentioned in Genesis.

Abraham was almost 100 years old when God made this most important covenant with him. Abraham was not able to fathom such an astounding announcement because he had already come to look upon Ishmael as the promised heir (Gen. 15:4). He was overwhelmed with wonder and great sadness when he surmised that God had rejected Ishmael. He was unaware that God would bless both Ishmael and Isaac, and use them according to His sovereign will and good purpose (Rev. 4:11).

Abraham was shaken by this unexpected announcement. He fell on his face, as he usually does when talking to God in prayer, and interceded fervently for his beloved son. He said to the Lord, "Oh, that Ishmael might live before You!" (Gen. 17:18). No one really knows how long Abraham agonized in prayer on behalf of his only son. Many of us are able to identify with Abraham's trial of faith, but most of us cannot understand the reason God allows His servants to suffer under the most grueling circumstances.

I believe God loves to test our faith in order to help us develop our spiritual growth. After having been tested, the believer would become stronger and more mature in his faith and ready to meet new challenges in life. Suffering may be likened to fire. Fire accomplishes two main objectives: it destroys and it purifies. Suffering roots out impurities in the believer, purifies our character, and confirms us as children of God (Heb. 12:7). Through suffering we realize that God is in total control of our lives, and without Him we "can do nothing" (John 15:5).

God commanded Abraham to seal the covenant with blood, with the sign of circumcision. Abraham "received the sign of circumcision, a seal of the righteousness of the faith which he had while still uncircumcised, that he might be the father of all those who believe, though they are uncircumcised, that righteousness might be imputed [transferred] to them also" (Rom. 4:11). Circumcision was a symbol which prefigured the atoning blood of Christ, because "all things are purged with blood, and without shedding of blood there is no remission" (Heb. 9:22). Paul clarifies this truth by declaring that a genuine believer is one who has been circumcised spiritually. In other words, circumcision in the flesh saves no one, but "circumcision is that of the heart, in the Spirit, and not in the letter, whose praise is not from men but from God" (Rom. 2:29). Abraham, Ishmael, and "every male among the men of Abraham's house" were all circumcised (Gen. 17:23).

The rite of circumcision was not restricted to Abraham and his people. It was also practiced in Canaan and other parts of the world. God wanted to seal the covenant (agreement) between Him and Abraham with blood, which is a symbol of being "justified by His blood, we shall be saved from wrath through Him" (Rom. 5:9). Remember that Abraham's salvation occurred long before the covenant of circumcision had been established. Circumcision was simply a sign of an inward and perpetual relationship with Jehovah. Abraham and Ishmael were the first believers to participate in the rite of circumcision in order to confirm their saving faith.

God had predetermined to use Ishmael in a historical role, and Isaac in a prophetic role. Each one of them was equally loved by both God and Abraham, but they were appointed different roles to play in the dispensation of the Abrahamic covenant. Since this book is mainly concerned to bring to light the untold story of God's love for Ishmael and his descendants, I will not expound upon Isaac's prophetic role. A multitude of books and commentaries have exalted Isaac and belittled Ishmael, and were unable to present a balanced view of God's indiscriminate love for the two sons of Abraham. Such unbalanced presentation gave rise to the propagation of a racial gospel and the promulgation of political theology.

This was the first severe trial for Ishmael, but not the last. At the very moment that his father conveyed to him the presumably shocking and disappointing news, Ishmael's countenance was marked by a feeling of vexation, and he became angry and deeply depressed. Anyone in Ishmael's perplexing situation would have reacted at least with much the same chagrin and indignation. Ishmael's rightful anger was an outgrowth of his inability to comprehend how his loving and honorable father could deprive him of his legal inheritance.

I suppose that all the human actors of this exciting drama were mainly concerned with their own interest and self-preservation. This is a common human behavioral pattern. People act and react according to their selfish desires and expectations, without giving careful attention and consideration to God's wondrous plan for their lives.

I can see Ishmael hopping on his favorite Arabian horse and riding it without a saddle. One can assume that he had acquired this habit through his childhood upbringing. He was trained to race the desert wind on his horse in pursuit of gazelles and any of the various antelopes and other desert animals. However, this time Ishmael was running away to find solace in the quietness of the desert and to meditate on his seeming misfortune. Little did he know that God was planning to bless him beyond measure. Ishmael is a type of the flesh (Gal. 4:23–24), and we can identify with his human emotion and impetuousness.

While Ishmael's young mind was trying to figure out the present predicament, and at the same time that his parents were praying for him, God intervened abruptly and said to Abraham, "And as for Ishmael, I have heard you. Behold, I have blessed him, and will make him fruitful, and will multiply him exceedingly. He shall beget twelve princes, and I will make him a great nation" (Gen. 17:20).

I was converted to faith in Christ on September 11, 1955, from the Druze religion, a mystical offshoot of the Shiite sect of Islam. My conversion took place near Princeton, New Jersey. From that moment until now, I have never heard a sermon nor have I ever read anything related to Ishmael becoming a great nation. Western biblical scholars seem to have downplayed the promises bestowed upon Ishmael and his descendants. It is bewildering to me how these commentators and speakers were able to justify their conditioned prejudice by distorting the truth and misleading the public into believing that God favors Isaac and his descendants over Ishmael and his peoples. No wonder that such biblical teaching is "making the word of God of no effect through your tradition which you have handed down" (Mark 7:13).

Let us remember that God created both Ishmael and Isaac. He loved both of them equally. He gave them eternal salvation, but He chose each one of them to play a different role according to His sovereign plan for the human race.

Unmistakably, when the Lord opened Abraham's heart to heed the things which were spoken to him concerning the distinct roles of Ishmael and Isaac (Gen. 17:19–21), it became clear to him that his unborn son was chosen as a vessel prophetically so the Promised Seed, "who is Christ," should come to redeem us from the curse of the law (Gal. 3:16). And Ishmael was chosen as a vessel historically in order to fulfill God's purpose for the Semitic Arabs (Gen. 16:10; 17:20; 21:13, 18).

God's plan for all the peoples of the earth is to "be fruitful and multiply; fill the earth" (Gen. 1:28; 9:1, 7; 10:32). It is emphatically clear that God loves the human race, and He is "not willing that any should perish but that all should come to repentance" (2 Peter 3:9; cf. Acts 17:26–31).

With this manner of illumination, Abraham understood the balance between prophecy and salvation. Undoubtedly, he came to the conclusion that salvation is more important than prophecy. In fact, salvation is the most important doctrine in the Bible. However, in order that salvation might be appropriated, prophecy must first be fulfilled—the Redeemer must come. This particular prophecy has already been fulfilled.

After such a joyful discernment, Abraham was ready to receive his angry son with an exuberant welcome. He was anxiously awaiting Ishmael's return from the desert in order to share these glad tidings with him. Abraham was probably sitting outside the tent door in the cool of the day, when he saw his discouraged son coming on his horse from a great way off. Soon after, Ishmael was seen pulling his horse toward his father's tent with his countenance fallen.

Abraham's camp was filled with enthusiasm and great anticipation, when Ishmael fell in his father's outstretched arms. He looked faint and famished. His father comforted him with hugs and kisses, and took him inside the tent, where his mother and Sarah were waiting to greet him. Apparently, Sarah loved Ishmael and considered him still to be her legal son, despite the fact that she would soon have her own child. Hagar had prepared a roasted lamb and venison meat with homemade bread. She baked the wheat and barley bread by rolling out the dough until it became thin enough. Then it was stuck on the side of the oven, where it baked in just a few seconds. After this delicious meal, Ishmael was ready to hear all that his father wanted to tell him.

As Ishmael listened with great interest to his father's most recent encounter with God, and as he began to understand what was said about him and Isaac, his heart swelled with pride and joy. No doubt he was looking forward to having a younger brother with whom he could play and socialize and train in the activities which he knew best.

Those who have been blessed with more than one child know that the eldest child influences the younger one, whether it be for good or bad. Ishmael was endowed with many good qualities, and he had inherited some of his parents' genetic and cultural traits which were commendable. Abraham and his peoples were predicting a harmonious future for both Isaac and Ishmael, with the belief that Ishmael's birthright would entitle him to remain the legal heir to his father's house.

A few months before the birth of Isaac, God appeared again to Abraham and alerted him of His determination to destroy Sodom and Gomorrah "because their sin is very grievous" (Gen. 18:20). The grievous sins of the two cities were homosexuality and sodomy. The Scripture clearly warns that the Almighty will surely bring terrible judgment and doom upon all the inhabitants of any country who are involved in such hateful sins (Gen. 19).

What is so interesting to us here is the fact that Ishmael must have seen the same "Angel of the Lord," who spoke face-to-face with his mother, and now He was visiting his father. The young man helped his father and Sarah in the preparation and serving the food and refreshments to the Lord and the two angels (Gen. 18:1–8). Moreover, I believe that Ishmael saw the searing flames and black smoke ascending from the two sinful cities, because Sodom and Gomorrah were about eighteen miles from his father's home at Mamre (Hebron). The young Ishmael had seen God and witnessed many other amazing events that helped shape his character. He also learned obedience and absolute trust in his God. Now he was ready to face the challenges of life.

When all has been said and done, and the dust seemed to have settled, Sarah gave birth to Isaac, meaning laughter. Her joy knew no bounds when she held him in her arms and nursed him in her old age. She was ninety years old, ten years younger than her husband. Abraham had the privilege of circumcising "his son Isaac when he was eight days old" (Gen. 21:4). When Isaac grew, his mother weaned him, and as it was customary, his father "made a great feast on the same day that Isaac was weaned" (Gen. 21:8).

No one can truly understand the unconscious mental processes of another person, let alone understanding his own. The human mind and emotions are a complex dynamic system. People usually choose to follow in the very steps of the behavior patterns their parents programmed into their brains in early childhood. It seems as though Sarah had not forgotten how sterile women were stigmatized with shame and disrespect. Now with the arrival of her own son, Sarah's dormant fleshly jealousy coupled with her hidden feelings of contempt toward Hagar were revived.

There are no recorded instances in the Old Testament of Ishmael's persecuting Isaac. One does not need to possess a prolific imagination in order to see Sarah ruminating a great deal over memories of Hagar's romantic involvement with Abraham. Any woman of moral character in a similar situation would have internalized some resentment toward Hagar. Consequently, Sarah was forced to repress her feelings and conquer her wrath for more than sixteen years by bringing them reluctantly under mental and emotional subjection.

Isaac was probably three years old when he was weaned. In the midst of the festivities, Sarah's fury was aroused by Ishmael's "mocking" Isaac. According to *Young's Analytical Concordance of the Bible*, the Hebrew word for "mocking," or "to mock," is *tsachaq*, meaning to play with. *Tsachaq* is an intensive form of the verb on which the word Isaac is built. To paraphrase the *Wycliffe Bible Commentary*, Ishmael was not scoffing or persecuting Isaac, but he was merely playing with his younger brother. When the apostle Paul intimated that Ishmael "persecuted" Isaac, he was using Sarah's point of view to prove his argument that salvation can only be received by faith alone. He was using a historical fact to illustrate a spiritual truth.

As we approach the climax of the story in this chapter, we come now to the most misconstrued and abused Scripture in relation to the Arabs and Muslims. During my seminary training, I was conditioned with the belief that God favored Isaac over Ishmael in every possible way. The proof text used to support this argument was quoted from the allegory found in Galatians 4:21–31. What made this instruction believable to me is that I was taught that God Himself drove out Hagar and Ishmael from Abraham's house. I was told that God said, "Cast out the bondwoman and her son, for the son of the bondwoman shall not be heir with the son of the freewoman" (Gal. 4:30).

I was utterly convinced that God Himself expelled both Hagar and Ishmael, mainly because they were inferior to the chosen Sarah and Isaac. This is exactly how most of the evangelicals and their counterparts in the Western world look at both the Arabs and Jews theologically and racially. They fail to see them as the Lord and Savior, Jesus Christ, sees them. Even Peter, the Hebrew, said that God does not show partiality. "But in every nation whoever fears Him and works righteousness is accepted by Him" (Acts 10:35).

The logic behind this widely held mythical interpretation of Galatians 4:30 seems credible because the apostle Paul was writing under the superintending of the Holy Spirit, and not of his own "private interpretation" (2 Peter 1:20–21). I personally believe in the plenary inspiration and inerrancy of the Bible, but such a deductive reasoning and teaching concerning God Himself ordering the casting out of the mother and her son is totally out of context and completely erroneous.

As a matter of fact, God never said that Ishmael and his mother must be thrown out of Abraham's house—Sarah did. Only God knew Sarah's real motive when she told her husband, "Cast out this bondwoman and her son; for the son of this bondwoman shall not be heir with my son, namely with Isaac" (Gen. 21:10). The tension in this statement betrays an angry and bitter spirit. Sarah had previously suffered much from jealousy of Hagar's youthful beauty and fertility. And although she had loved Ishmael as her own son in the past, she could no longer allow him to remain the legal heir. She feared that Abraham would still give his older son the bulk of the inheritance. Again she became hysterical and insisted upon the expulsion of Hagar and her son.

There is a generally accepted belief among Christians that since the Bible is inspired and inerrant, and since the apostle Paul recorded the exact words God wanted him to record, therefore, God Himself commanded the casting out of "the bondwoman and her son" (Gal. 4:30). The Bible is inerrant, but God did not Himself say everything that was said in the Bible. Inerrancy means that all things that were recorded by the inspired human writers in the sixty-six books of the Bible are free from error, from start to finish in the original manuscripts.

Many events took place in the Bible that were initiated by human actors and not by God. However, all the events that took place in the Bible were recorded without error. For instance, God did not inspire Sarah to punish Hagar and her son, but He inspired Moses and Paul to record the story without error. God did not inspire Satan to say what he said, but He inspired the writers to record the exact words and deeds of Satan without a mistake. God did not inspire King David to kill Uriah and marry his wife, Bathsheba, but He inspired the writer of the second book of Samuel to record the story without error.

There are many more examples in the Bible where people acted according to their selfish desires, as Sarah did, and their actions and utterances were recorded without error. This is called *inerrancy*.

Several Christian friends have told me on many occasions that they believe the Bible "from cover to cover." I usually say to them that I am very glad for their uncompromising faith in Christ and His Word, the Bible, but they should make sure to know and understand what really took place between the two covers of the Bible.

It is interesting to know how Paul uses Hagar in the allegory in order to emphasize the traditionally accepted belief that she is inferior to Sarah. The use of Hagar as inferior to

Sarah is an established Jewish tradition, not only in rabbinic literature but also in many other publications as well. Whether she is the slave woman serving the free mistress, or the daughter of Pharaoh given as a slave, Hagar and her descendants are still looked upon as representatives of a class of servants which is below the status of Sarah and her descendants.

Hence Sarah's request to cast out Hagar and Ishmael has become a gospel truth and a divine command. This was and still is the contention of many preachers and others, and remains the chief concern of Western political theology in order to show the superiority of Sarah over Hagar and the worthiness of Isaac over Ishmael.

Conversely, in interpreting Galatians 4:21–31, we need to study carefully and prayerfully Genesis 16 through 21 to hear the true version of the Sarah–Hagar story. As noted previously in this study, the picture of Hagar and Ishmael in Genesis is very different from that of the allegory in Galatians.

Hagar's story is a haunting one. It foreshadows the story of Jacob wandering in the wilderness because there was nowhere else to go and no one to whom to turn, until God revealed Himself to him and transformed his life. The difference between the two stories is that Hagar's story is about human suffering and bondage. God used her to teach us that only through Jesus Christ can we escape from eternal bondage and suffering. God revealed Himself to Hagar, as He did to Jacob, and set her free from human bondage, but not from earthly suffering (Gal. 3:28).

Lest we forget, Sarah loved Ishmael as her own son before the birth of Isaac. Sarah's change of attitude came as a result of Hagar's intimate relationship with Abraham, coupled with Ishmael's determination to claim his legal right to the inheritance.

Hagar—Free at Last

We will soon see how the brief account of the departure of Hagar, and her journey through the desert, turned out to be one of the most beautiful and touching pictures of the patriarchal love of God.

In the *Antiquities of the Jews*, Flavius Josephus commented on this issue:

> As for Sarah, she at first loved Ismael, who was born of her own handmaid Hagar, with an affection not inferior to that of her own son, for he was brought up, in order to succeed in the government; but when she herself had borne Isaac, she was not willing that Ismael should be brought up with him. . . . she therefore persuaded Abraham to send him and his mother to some distant country.[1]

Paul quoted Sarah in the allegory of Galatians 4:30, without agreeing with her selfish and harsh motive, because he was striving to corroborate his assertion that the things of Christ are much greater than those concerning the law. He did this by mentioning Hagar and Sarah so that from such a comparison he might make his point clear.

Allegory should not be taken literally. The dictionary defines allegory as a figurative treatment of one subject under the guise of another. In other words, allegory is a symbolic narrative of a historical fact used to illustrate a spiritual truth. Paul symbolically used this historical episode of Isaac and Ishmael, Hagar and Sarah, to support his argument about the legalistic religiosity of the Jewish zealotry as opposed to the freedom of the new covenant of grace instituted by our Lord Jesus Christ.

Richard Longenecker wrote on the Pauline hermeneutic regarding the controversial passage of Galatians 4:21–31, and concluded that it is "a highly allegorical representation of Old Testament history."[2] This, he believes, is the case because the apostle Paul "definitely goes beyond the literal and primary sense of the narrative to insist upon hidden and symbolic meanings in the words."[3]

Upon the incessant demand of Sarah to banish Hagar and Ishmael from Abraham's dwellings, "the matter was very displeasing in Abraham's sight because of his son" (Gen. 21:11). This harsh treatment of Ishmael was extremely painful to Abraham. Sarah's treatment of Hagar, from the beginning until now, is indicative of her choleric temperament. A choleric person loves to control and manipulate other people. Abraham's temperament was absolutely phlegmatic, because he was eager to please others and tried to endure testings patiently and prudently.

Almost every time I am teaching a seminar on the topic under discussion, many ask me the following question: "Did not God agree with Sarah to cast out Hagar and Ishmael?" To substantiate their argument, they appeal to Genesis 21:12, when God said to Abraham, "Do not let it be displeasing in your sight because of the lad or because of your bondwoman. Whatever Sarah has said to you, listen to her voice; for in Isaac your seed shall be called."

I ordinarily answer this question with a question. I ask them if they truly believe that God would agree with Sarah's selfish motive and sinful desire to cast out Hagar and her son, and also to greedily deprive Ishmael from his legal right to the inheritance? The answer of the majority is an emphatic *no!* And sometimes a few people argue with me from a subjective point of view, based on their preconceived theological persuasion.

They ask again, if God did not agree with Sarah, why then did He tell Abraham to listen to his wife? God is a peacemaker; He wanted to allow the two mothers and their sons to live independently from each other, in order to fulfill His foreordained sovereign plan for the two Semitic races. Since Ishmael was old enough to face the challenges of life, with the help of God and his mother, God was ready to lead him to the wilderness to prepare him for his historical role.

Despite the fact that Abraham was tested before, this trial was unbearable to him because he loved Ishmael very much. It is difficult to picture mentally the scene outside and inside the tent, and to describe the morbid mood of all concerned the day prior to Ishmael's departure. I believe that Hagar and her son were under God's providential care, when "Abraham rose early in the morning, and took bread and a skin of water. . . . he gave it and the boy to Hagar, and sent her away. Then she departed and wandered in the Wilderness of Beersheba" (Gen. 21:14).

Abraham's grief was comforted by God when he was told to let them go and was assured that each of his two sons would have an important place in life. Both of them would father great nations, but in Isaac the Promised Seed "shall be called" (Gen. 21:12; cf. Gal. 3:16).

Abraham had experienced God's providential care before. He knew that Ishmael and Hagar would be protected and provided for in the wilderness. I believe this is the reason Abraham gave them only some bread and a goatskin bottle of water, and sent them away toward Beer-sheba. Beer-sheba was on the border of Egypt and was about fifty miles south of Jerusalem and more than twenty-five miles south of Hebron.

I have been fascinated by Hagar's unusual character because the more I delve into her life-style the more she shines brightly as a model of submission to authority, faith, endurance, tenacity, and motherly love. Hagar's stimulating and provocative story forces us to remember the hopeless and helpless who are suffering everywhere in the world at the hands of selfish and cruel individuals. God cares for them and wishes that every one of them should come to know Him, as Hagar did. Donald Grey Barnhouse wrote regarding this, saying, "We see here that God never fails to see what is going on and that He is vitally interested in everything that touches one of His creatures."[4]

Hagar and her teenage son were overcome by fatigue and thirst in that arid region. She withdrew a little distance so she would not see Ishmael's lingering hurt and possible death. She acted as any loving mother would act under such an event. She "lifted her voice and wept." She wept bitterly and loudly, not only for her son's adverse circumstances, but also for her own. It was not the ideal time for her to remember all that God had promised, while she and her son were suffering from starvation.

When everything seemed hopeless in Hagar's mind, the Angel of God spoke to her again: "What ails you, Hagar? Fear not, for God has heard the voice of the lad where he is. Arise, lift up the lad and hold him with your hand, for I will make him a great nation" (Gen. 21:17–18). God came to Hagar's rescue in the past when she was in a similar predicament, and now He called her from heaven to reinforce and reassure her of the immutable promises which He had already made to her and to Abraham concerning their son (Gen. 16:10; 17:20; 21:13).

God appeared to Hagar and not to Sarah because Hagar was both a slave and a fugitive. I believe that God did this to show us that He has a special interest in such people. Of course, He is also interested in people from all walks of life, but since the poor and the disinherited are treated badly in this life, God is especially attentive to their cries.

Ishmael and his mother cried out to their God in distress, and when they did, they discovered that He was not far from them. This had been God's method of deliverance. God rescues those who fervently cry out for help and who seek Him with all their heart (Jer. 29:13). The inspired King David wrote, "This poor man cried out, and the Lord heard him, and saved him out of all his troubles" (Ps. 34:6). The problem is that many people love to feed on their miseries rather than to cry out to God for help. Even King David cried out to the Lord with all humility. He said, "I sought the Lord, and He heard me, and delivered me from all my fears" (Ps. 34:4).

The Angel of the Lord, and the Angel of God, who spoke twice to Hagar, is actually a preincarnate manifestation of our Lord and Savior, Jesus Christ, the Second Person of the Trinity. The fact that the word *angel* means "messenger," does not necessarily denote someone belonging to the order of created spiritual beings. H. C. Leupold wrote in his *Exposition of Genesis,*

> The Angel of the Lord is not a created being but the Divine Being Himself; for
> 1. He explicitly identifies Himself with Yahweh on various occasions.
> 2. Those to whom He makes His presence known recognize Him as divine.
> 3. The Biblical writers call Him Yahweh.
> 4. The doctrine here implied of a plurality of persons in the Godhead is in complete accordance with earlier foreshadowing.
> 5. The organic unity of Scripture would be broken if it could be proved that the central point in the Old Testament revelation was a creature-angel, while that of the New is the incarnation of the God-Man.[5]

It has been reported that one of the early church fathers, stated, "Anyone who tries to fathom the Trinity fully will lose his mind, and anyone who denies the Trinity will surely lose his soul." This is a true statement because no one is able to comprehend everything the Bible teaches. There are so many truths in the Bible which we ought to understand, and we must occupy ourselves with them in order to reach maturity in the faith and to walk with God with an obedient spirit, like Abraham and Hagar did.

The first time Hagar decided to run away from Sarah, she was commanded to go back. God wanted Ishmael to be raised in a godly home until he was old enough to be separated from Isaac. This conjecture harmonizes much better with the holy character and holy nature of the Almighty, and also with the whole story of Hagar and Ishmael, than that of other interpretations which have been published.

Hagar and Ishmael were provided with plenty of fresh and flowing water in the wilderness, a symbol of a new start and a new chapter in life. Then "his mother took a wife for him from the land of Egypt" (Gen. 21:21). It is interesting to note here that Ephraim and Manasseh, the two sons of Joseph, were born in Egypt from an Egyptian mother.

Prior to Abraham's death, I am sure that Ishmael visited his father several times, and it does not appear that any long alienation existed between him and Isaac; for when their father died, the two brothers "buried him in the cave of Machpelah" (Gen. 25:9). That must have been an exciting scene to behold. Isaac and his people side by side with Ishmael and his whole body of followers and allies.

Probably before the death of his father, Ishmael was called to the deathbed of Abraham, given that good relations had been kept up between Isaac and Ishmael. God had apparently blessed Ishmael with much more land and wealth than what his father could have given him, because "God was with the lad," before and after he was disinherited, and now God was ready to make of him "a great nation" (Gen. 21:18-21)!

"The eyes of the Lord, which scan to and fro throughout the whole earth" (Zech. 4:10) are searching for individuals who are willing to submit and totally surrender their ethnic pride and prejudice to the reconditioning power of the Holy

107

Spirit. I believe, then, and only then, the Holy Spirit may sweep across the nations in supernatural power, convicting and convincing sinners of their total depravity. However, as long as the majority of televangelists and Bible teachers continue to propagate a political and racial theology, a multitude of Arabs and others will not experience the eternal love of Christ, as both Hagar and Ishmael did.

5

The Making of
a Great Nation

There is no doubt in my mind that the promises made to Abraham and Hagar concerning Ishmael becoming "a great nation" were mostly fulfilled with the historic golden age of Islam.

According to my understanding of Scripture, God elects peoples and nations in three different ways. He elects individuals and nations to fulfill His sovereign prophetic plan. He elects individuals and nations in order to fulfill their historical roles. And He elects only individuals so that they may be justified by faith alone, whereby they will be made free from the penalty of guilt for the sin of unbelief (John 1:29). The most important aspect of election is the latter one, mainly because it is directly related to God's grace and mercy regarding eternal salvation.

In agreement with the prophet Daniel, and with the apostle John, "That the Most High rules in the kingdom of men, gives it to whomever He will, and. . . . does according to His will in the army of heaven and among the inhabitants of the earth. No one can restrain His hand or say to Him, 'What have You done?'" (Dan. 4:17, 35). In other words, God is sovereign; He rules the whole creation with His awesome power and wisdom. He has elected people from all walks of life, and put "into their hearts to fulfill His purpose . . . until the words of God are fulfilled!" (Rev. 17:17) With this in mind, let us contemplate how and why God initiated the rise of Islam and gave the Arabs much physical wealth.

Let me remind the reader at this juncture that the purpose of the book is initially to enlighten Western understanding on the character and historical contributions of the Arabs from a positive approach, in order to help remove some of the negative standardized conceptions about the Arabs.

The reader may observe that I am writing subjectively. This is a fair observation, because man has always been conditioned by the religious, political, and sociological views of his ethnic heritage. These views mold his attitudes, shape his responses and beliefs, and guide his thoughts and actions. In this sense no one is able to verbalize or to write objectively without being subjective. Dr. William Sanford La-Sor, who wrote the foreword to the works of Josephus, said: "In all fairness we must add that even Josephus was a Jew and was doubtless writing to honor his fellow countrymen and to defend Judaism."[1]

A Brief Introduction to Islam

The appeal of Islam as a universal religion is based on its striking simplicity and practicality. From its inception, it has been vigorously and successfully missionary. It has made exclusive claims of truth and applied its principles to the peoples of all nations and races.

Islam, in Arabic, denotes submission, specifically to the will of Allah. *Allah* is the Arabic word for "God." Although Hagar is not mentioned by name in the Qur'an, the doctrine of total submission to God could be traced to her encounter with the Most High (Gen. 16:13). Islam stresses the unity and sovereignty of Allah. However, since Allah is remote and invisible, man can only submit to His will and not to His Person.

Islam is a way of life with a clear set of universally binding beliefs which designate every aspect of conduct. In spite of division among its adherents, Islam unifies every Muslim and binds them to each other with a common faith and unites them around certain explicit tenets and practices.

Islam teaches that the Prophet Muhammad is the seal of God's prophets, the last messenger who brought God's final revelation to the world. During his ministry Muhammad confronted paganism with great courage and integrity, and unified Arabia in submission to the will of Allah. His assertion of the oneness of God and other logical and practical teachings laid the groundwork for Muslim world mission.

The Qur'an is understood by Muslims to contain the last precise words of Allah, which were revealed to Muhammad in Arabic by the angel Gabriel. The Qur'an, about two-thirds the length of the New Testament, is divided into 114 surahs (chapters), and its exclusive content is instruction from Allah.

For instance, the Qur'an teaches that human beings are utterly responsible to Allah for all that they do or say. Disobedience can be forgiven through confession and prayer directly to Allah, without the help of intercessors. Allah is the creator and sustainer of His creation, and He defines right and wrong by decree.

The Qur'an specifically teaches that Allah is not three, but one. All other sins are insignificant compared with the blasphemy of associating another deity with Allah. Thus, there is no need for the incarnation and the atonement for sin. Only submission to the will of Allah is the norm for the Muslim to secure eternal salvation.

The Qur'an teaches that Jesus (Isa) was born of a virgin named Mariam (Mary). He was a man and a slave of Allah, a comforter to believers, but absolutely he was not God or the Son of God. Jesus was not crucified, but ascended into heaven from whence he will return to complete his unfinished mission and eventually die. An empty tomb awaits him in Medina, Saudi Arabia.

I would like to insert here a fact that has been overlooked by many historians in the West. People who are unfamiliar with Islam may be surprised to know that it is a tolerant and compassionate religion. For example, Islam has shown more compassion toward the Jews and others than has Christendom. There has never been an Islamic Inquisition or a Holocaust equivalent to that of Hitler's regime. Islamic countries have welcomed Jewish refugees fleeing from the horror and savagery of Christendom. Jewish scholars were able to reach high positions during the golden age of Islam and also to enjoy the unmatched hospitality of their blood relatives, the Arabs.

Those who are interested in presenting a tender Christian witness to Muslims should not criticize nor disparage the Qur'an, nor should they try to argue with Muslims. God said that He loves the human race and He desires that we do likewise. But how can we love anyone if we do not know the person and understand his or her cultural upbringing? The Lord Jesus encouraged us to become peacemakers, not debaters. "Blessed are the peacemakers, for they shall be called sons of God" (Matt. 5:9).

The Rise of Islam

God promised to make of Ishmael "a great nation," and to multiply his "descendants exceedingly, so that they shall not be counted for multitude" (Gen. 16:10; 17:20; 21:13, 18). Ishmael and his twelve sons did not become a great nation during their lifetimes, but their descendants did fulfill the promise historically with the rise of Islam.

Arab genealogists assert that Muhammad's ancestry can

From Ishmael to Muhammad

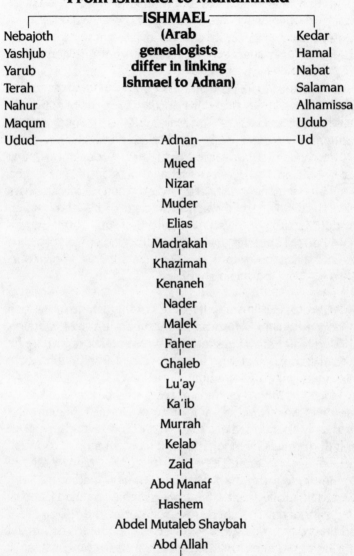

ISHMAEL
(Arab genealogists differ in linking Ishmael to Adnan)

Nebajoth		Kedar
Yashjub		Hamal
Yarub		Nabat
Terah		Salaman
Nahur		Alhamissa
Maqum		Udub
Udud	Adnan	Ud

Adnan
|
Mued
|
Nizar
|
Muder
|
Elias
|
Madrakah
|
Khazimah
|
Kenaneh
|
Nader
|
Malek
|
Faher
|
Ghaleb
|
Lu'ay
|
Ka'ib
|
Murrah
|
Kelab
|
Zaid
|
Abd Manaf
|
Hashem
|
Abdel Mutaleb Shaybah
|
Abd Allah
|
Muhammad

be traced to Ishmael. This assertion is based on the law of blood-revenge, which required the people to trace their ancestry back four generations. This law was handed down on the genealogical records sequentially from one generation to the other.

We leave Ishmael now and start with Muhammad to see how God used the Arabs historically. Prophet Muhammad was born around A.D. 571 at Makkah (Mecca), Saudi Arabia. *Muhammad* means "highly praised," a name given to more Muslim sons than any other. His father, Abdullah, meaning "slave of God," died before Muhammad's birth. His mother, Aminah, meaning "trustworthy," died when he was six years old. The orphan child was in the care of his grandfather, Abdul Mutalib, who also died, and the duty of raising Muhammad fell upon his uncle, Abu-Talib, who could not afford to keep his nephew for long. The young lad was obliged to earn his livelihood as a shepherd.

At the age of twenty-five, Muhammad married a rich widow, Khadijah, who was fifteen years his senior. He attended to her affairs in southern Arabia and Syria, where he became conversant with a monk named Bahira, who gave him much information about Christianity.

Placed in affluent circumstances by his marriage to Khadijah, who was from the same tribe of Qureish, Muhammad gradually abandoned commercial enterprises and gave himself up to religious meditation and contemplation, to which he may have been influenced by a relative. Many Arabs of Muhammad's day had forsaken idolatry and were converted first to Judaism, then to Christianity, but had failed to find satisfaction in either. However, during the rise of Islam and thereafter many Arabs remained faithful to their belief in Christ.

Chirography, or handwriting, had only been introduced

into Arabia a short time, though Arabian poetry was highly cultivated, when Muhammad received the revelation of the Qur'an. Retired in solitude near a little cave called Gharat al-Hīra, on a hill outside of Makkah, Muhammad reviewed the various systems of religion known to him by oral tradition in order to adapt from them his own belief.

It was then that Muhammad heard a voice commanding: "Recite thou in the name of thy Lord who created. . . ."[2] The night that he received his call was later named "the Night of Power" (laylat al-qadr). It is believed that the angel Gabriel had appeared to him and in the name of Allah commanded Muhammad to recite, to preach, and to spread the true religion throughout the world. Since Muhammad could not write nor probably read well enough, his recitation of the Qur'an from memory in perfect Arabic is cited as miraculous, and of course, gave credence to his message.

Meanwhile, in three years only fourteen converts believed his message. Among them was the high-spirited Ali, Muhammad's cousin, who helped in the ultimate success of the new religion. In the fourth year of his mission, Muhammad made a public declaration of his faith. He preached against idolatry and warned the people that unless they repented from worshipping gods other than Allah, they could have no happiness in this life nor eternal salvation in the life hereafter.

God hates idolatry, and I believe that "Mohammed appeared at a time when the Church had become Paganized with the worship of Images, Relics, Martyrs, Mary, and the Saints. In a sense Mohammedanism was a revolt against the Idolatry of the Christian world; a judgment on a corrupt and degenerate Church."[3]

As it was then, the Christian world still is living largely in whoredom and lukewarmness (Rev. 3:16). Assyria was used of God as the rod of His anger to discipline the Jews for

115

provoking Him to wrath, and Islam is being used presently in many ways to provoke the lethargic church to jealousy concerning world evangelization. On many occasions some of my Christian friends want to know the reason for Islam's success and growth worldwide. It is because the Muslims are obeying their prophet's command—they are faithfully and relentlessly spreading their faith by word and deed. Meanwhile, the Christians are disputing among themselves and criticizing other religions.

Islam has close affinities with both Judaism and Christianity, but Muhammad gradually broke away from them. Islam developed into an independent religion with a distinct system of belief. In his message, the prophet was as bold in his declarations as any of the Hebrew prophets of the Old Testament: "Allah is one God. He is the creator and sustainer of the universe. He will reward the faithful with eternal salvation, and will punish in hell those who disobey Him."

Although Muhammad was considered by Muslims to be God's legitimate vice-regent and supreme ruler on earth before his death, he led a humble and unpretentious life in a clay house consisting of a few rooms. "He was often seen mending his own clothes and was at all times within the reach of his people."[4] The Qur'an contains a wide spectrum of laws governing almost every aspect of life. On behalf of the weak, the orphan, the slave, and the oppressed, Muhammad had special care for them, and we find the legislation of him who was himself once a poor orphan especially benevolent.[5]

Muhammad married about twelve wives, fewer than David and Solomon. He married some of them for political reasons, one of whom was a Christian Copt by the name of Mary. Mary bore him a son, Ibrahim, who died in infancy and was mourned bitterly by his father. Muhammad had only one surviving daughter by Khadijah, named Fātimah, who became the wife of Ali. The Shiite sect of Islam descended from this marriage.

According to the Qur'an, the word *Islam* is derived from the verb *aslamā* (Surah 37:103), meaning "submission or surrender to the will of Allah." The Qur'an teaches that Abraham surrendered to the will of Allah by his attempt to sacrifice Ishmael, not Isaac. This "was evidently the act that provided Muhammad with the name for the new faith."[6] In the doctrine of total submission to the will of Allah lies the simplicity and strength of Islam. The Muslims enjoy their faith with resignation and contentment unknown to other religions.

Shortly after the death of Muhammad in A.D. 632, Roman rule was put to an end as the enthusiastic followers of the prophet swarmed out from the Arabian Peninsula to sweep the Fertile Crescent. Later they pushed east as far as the Indus River and west through North Africa and Spain, where they ruled from the eighth to the fifteenth century.

Islam is divided into two major groups: the Sunnites and the Shi'ites. The division resulted from disputes over the legitimate successor of prophet Muhammad as leader of the Muslims. The Shi'ites make up approximately 15 percent of the Muslim population, and they believe that Muhammad endorsed Ali as his successor. On the other hand, the Sunnites are the larger of the two major branches to evolve from Islam.

The Shi'ites and Sunnites also differ on many other points of law and theology. For instance, the Sunnites believe that there ought to be a division between civil and religious authority, whereas the Shi'ites believe that religious authority ought also to exercise political authority. The recent turmoil in Iran has been led by religious Shi'ite Muslims who exercise authority over civil and political matters.

The Golden Age of Islam

During the age of the Arab empire (632–1250), a major world civilization was added to the history of mankind. Arabic was then the *lingua franca*, and much intellectual activity and scientific research in practically every field of learning flourished. The torch of light was then carried by the Arabs, while Europe was enshrouded in the Dark Ages. The intellectual brilliance of that period reached its zenith and influenced and enriched other cultures.

Islam has been the only world religion to win great numbers of converts from Judaism, Christendom, and non-monotheistic religions. ''Countries that were once under the cross have taken up the crescent as their banner. Palestine, the home of Jesus and the Apostles, became a protectorate of the Arab Caliphs under Islam. Egypt, the center of theology from the time of Origen and Athanasius, came under the umbrella of Mecca, North Africa, where Augustine, Tertullian, Cyprian, and other apologists and theologians defended the faith (Jude 3), was incorporated into the world of Islam. Asia Minor (modern Turkey) was a hotbed of early church activity. The seven churches of the Book of Revelation were in Turkey as well as the cities of Antioch, Troas, Lystra, and Tarsus . . . an area now almost totally under strict Muslim domination.''[7]

The historical and geo-political importance of the Arab world has been featured by the abundance of scholarly works in many languages, while hardly any study has been done on the positive cultural contributions of the Arabs.

Between 685 and 705, the Islamic empire ''reached the meridian of its power and glory . . . stretching from the shores of the Atlantic Ocean and the Pyrenees to the Indus and the confines of China—an extent hardly rivalled in ancient times and unsurpassed in modern times . . . the reconquest . . . of North Africa and the acquisition of the largest European country ever held by Arabs—Spain."[8]

During this period, Arabic became the national language of the empire, the course of history in medieval Europe was radically changed, and a new way of thought was inaugurated. The establishment of this new order can be viewed as the golden age of Islam which was characterized by splendor and glory. People were converted to Islam from every race and creed; they became known as Arabs no matter what their nationality may originally have been. Anyone who professed Islam and wrote and spoke Arabic, regardless of his or her racial affiliation, became known as an Arab. The Muslims are erroneously called Moors by Western historians. The word *Moor* was originally used in Europe for Muslims of the mixed Berbers and Arabs living in northwest Africa.

In other words, not all the Arabs are Muslims, and not all the Muslims were Arabs originally. However, the term *Arab* has been used interchangeably with the word *Muslim* in this book, because all Muslims have been commanded by Muhammad to recite the Qur'an in Arabic. The Arab population is approximately two hundred million, and the number of Muslims around the world is nearly one billion.

Let us now try to learn briefly about the talent of the Arabs, and also make an attempt to formulate an appreciation of some of Islam's cultural contributions. History tells us that the descendants of Joktan, Ishmael, and Keturah have given the world one great prophet, theologians, philosophers, scientists, educators, poets, and others whose contributions were beneficial to mankind and truly encyclopedic, encompassing almost the whole spectrum of knowledge.

The contributions of the following Muslims to world civilization show merely the tip of the iceberg of Arabian culture. From Islam's point of view, the greatest contribution of the

Arabs to mankind is the Qur'an. This "miraculous revelation" to Muhammad in the spiritual realm was offered on the verbal level. Muhammad dictated the whole text of the Qur'an from memory and in perfect Arabic. Its rhetorical language has remained to this day the paragon in Arabic. The Qur'an is credited with saving the Arabic language from disintegrating into a variety of local dialects and preserving the unity of thought and expression. In this sense, the Qur'an belongs to the Christian Arabs as well as to all those who are associated with the same cultural background.

Al-Battani (d. A.D. 929) Al-Battani, a noted astronomer and mathematician, is credited with having improved upon Greek astronomical and mathematical works and for correcting the Ptolemaic tradition of astronomy. He discovered the notions of trigonometrical ratios as we use them today. "The science of trigonometry, like algebra and analytical geometry, was largely founded by Arabs."[9]

The stars provided a celestial map for the ancient nomads of Arabia and later on challenged the greatest minds of the Muslim world. To ancient civilizations, the starry sky was a mystifying astronomical phenomenon that even the best scholars could not explain. But of all the scholars who sought to unravel those mysteries, very few could be compared with those of the golden age of Islam. Mathematicians, philosophers, poets, theologians, historians, astronomers, physicians, linguists, and other scholars flocked to the Beit al-Hikmah (the House of Wisdom) in Baghdād or in Islamic Spain, in order to share their discoveries and then transmit their concepts and theories to Europe and the rest of the world.

Al-Battani showed, contrary to Ptolemy, that annular eclipses, in which a ring of light encircles the eclipsed portion, were possible and that the angular diameter of the sun was subject to variation. He corrected a number of previous miscalculations of planetary orbits and determined the correct and mean orbit of the sun. He also developed a theory related to the conditions of visibility of the new moon.

Al-Khwārizmi (d. A.D. 850) Al-Khwārizmi is said to have given algebra and algorithm their names. Much of the mathematical knowledge of medieval Europe was derived from his great works. Muhammad ibn Musa al-Khwārizmi was primarily a mathematician, but he also developed important astronomical tables. Along with other Muslim scholars, he built instruments to make observations and measurements and to calculate and test his data.

In connection with *beit al-Hikmah*, the Caliph erected at Baghdād an astronomical observatory under the directorship of an astronomer who was a converted Jew, called Sind ibn-Ali, who "not only made systematic observation of the celestial movements, but also verified with remarkably precise results all the fundamental elements of the obliquity of the ecliptic, the precession of the equinoxes, and the length of the solar year."[10]

Al-Fārābi (d. A.D. 950) Muhammad ibn-Muhammad ibn-Tārkhan abu-Nasr al-Fārābi (Alpharabius), a Turk, was educated by a Christian physician in Baghdād. He was a philosopher and a music theorist. His system of philosophy was a syncretism of Platonism and Aristotelianism. Apart from his commentaries on Greek philosophers, he wrote many psychological, political, and metaphysical works. Inspired by Plato's *Republic* and Aristotle's *Politics*, he wrote about an ideal city in which the object of association is the happiness of its citizens, and the sovereign is perfect morally and intellectually.[11]

Al-Fārābi became known after his death as the "second Aristotle." His metaphysical speculation influenced ibn Sīna

(Avicenna), who found in the works of al-Fārābi the fundamental notion of a distinction between existence and essence, the latter not implying necessarily that the former had to be given by God Himself. Al-Fārābi's method is largely dependent on Neoplatonism. Creation is emanation, and logic is considered to be a prerequisite to all science. Physics comprises all factual knowledge, including psychology, metaphysics, and ethics.

Al-Fārābi was a noted musician and is considered the greatest Arab music theorist. He is said to have played the *oud,* an ancestor of the guitar, like a magician. While performing at a large gathering, he first made the people laugh so much, then made them cry, and finally put them into a deep sleep.

Al-Ghazzāli (1058–1111) He was the best theologian of Islam and authored several important works on theology. His book, *Destruction of the Philosophers,* opposes the philosophical method of approaching metaphysics when it contradicts orthodox theology. His position influenced Thomas Aquinas and Pascal, and also affected Islamic thought. He is known in the West as Algazel.

Al-Ghazzāli started as a skeptic and became a mystic and then he ended as an orthodox Muslim. Philosophy is meaningful only as introduction to theology. His attitude coincides with Neoplatonic mysticism and is contradictory to Aristotelianism. He wrote an elaborate report on the doctrines of al-Fārābi and ibn Sīna, pointing out the self-contradictions of philosophers. Practically everything he wrote is based on theology.

Al-Kindi (ca. A.D. 801–873) Al-Kindi, abu-Yūsuf Ya'qūb ibn-Ishāq, was one of the three most renowned philosophers of the golden age of Islam. The other two were al-Fārābi, a

Turk, and ibn-Sīna, a Persian. Because of his Arabian descent, al-Kindi was called "the philosopher of the Arabs." He was eclectic in his treatment of philosophy and endeavored to combine both views of Plato and Aristotle. He also wrote on astronomy, astrology, geometry, arithmetic, music theory based on arithmetical principles, physics, medicine, psychology, meteorology, and politics. His works were truly encyclopedic.

In the field of theology he stressed the righteousness, sovereignty, as well as the unity of God. He believed that Allah revealed Himself in prophecy, which was a reasonable truth and the highest form of knowledge. He was the first to meet the violent hostility of the orthodox theologians, but he escaped without any harm.

Ibn-al-Haytham (A.D. 965–1039) He was a noted mathematician who introduced the idea that light rays emanate in straight lines in all directions from every point on a luminous surface. His works included astronomy, philosophy, and medicine. He was known in the medieval West as Alhazen. He influenced the scientific endeavors of Johannes Kepler and René Descartes.

His data in astronomy conflicted with that of Ptolemy. He argued that the Milky Way was quite far from the earth no matter what Aristotle said. He estimated the height of the earth's atmosphere at 52,000 meters, a meter being roughly three feet. Ibn-al-Haytham observed that the astronomic twilight begins when the negative height of the sun reaches 19 degrees. Since the atmosphere is about 50 kilometers (13 miles) and 52,000 meters (32 miles), al-Haytham was not far from the truth.

Muslim scientists revised and refined Ptolemy's catalog of stars. This catalog gave the positions of 1,022 stars, classified, as they are today, by magnitude or brightness.[12]

Ibn-Bājjah (d. A.D. 1138) The twelfth century was the golden century in philosophic thought in Muslim Spain. The century opened with abu-Bakr Muhammad ibn-Yahya ibn-Bājjah (Avenpace, or Avempace). He was a philosopher, physician, scientist, musician, and a noted lecturer and commentator on Aristotle. He influenced al-Ghazzāli and ibn-Rushd.

Ibn-Rushd (A.D. 1126–98) He was considered the greatest Muslim philosopher in Spain. He was born in Cordova as abu-al-Walid Muhammad ibn-Ahmad ibn-Rushd (Averroës). His family produced many theologians and judges. His chief philosophical work was his *Tahāfut al-Tahāfut* (the incoherence of the incoherence). This was a reply to al-Ghazzāli's attack on rationalism entitled *Tahāfut al-Falāsifah* (the incoherence of the Philosophers).[13]

Ibn-Rusd was more influential on Jewish and Christian thought than on Islam. He distinguished between faith and reason by pointing out that the two need not be reconciled because they did not conflict. He believed that philosophy is the highest form of inquiry.

From the latter part of the twelfth to the end of the sixteenth century, ibn-Rushd remained the dominant school in philosophic thought in Europe. He was a rationalist and claimed the right to submit everything to the judgment of reason. On the other hand, he was a strong believer in Allah, and he viewed creation as truly miraculous and evolutionary. "His writings became prescribed studies in the University of Paris and other institutions of higher learning."[14]

Ibn-Khaldūn (A.D. 1332–1406) Abd-al-Rahmān ibn-Khaldūn was born in Tunisia of Spanish-Arab extraction. His roots could be traced to an Arabian tribe of Hadramawt. He is considered by Arabs as the greatest historian and most reliable. He developed a consistent philosophy of history, as well as a unique method of writing in the areas of political economy and sociology. He played an important role in the politics of North Africa and Spain and served as his country's ambassador to Spain.

Ibn-Sīna (A.D. 980–1037) Abu-Ali al-Hussein ibn-Abdallah ibn-Sīna (Avicenna), a Persian, was the most illustrious name in Arabic medical annals. He was also a noted philosopher and poet. His work is truly encyclopedic. It includes over 200 titles dealing with medicine, philosophy, astronomy, geometry, theology, philology, and art. Of particular interest is his work in medical education. His studies became the approved textbook in the schools of Europe. In the last thirty years of the fifteenth century, his research in medicine passed through more than fifteen Latin editions and one Hebrew. In recent years a partial translation into English was made of his research in medicine. Avicenna's contributions in the field of medicine are enormous. Dr. William Osler commented during one of his lectures, "Avicenna's book has remained a medical bible for a longer period than any other work."[15]

God has truly fulfilled His promise to Abraham and Hagar by making of their son "a great nation." Obviously Abraham understood the promise and believed that God had elected Ishmael for a specific historical purpose (Gen. 17:20; 21:13). Having been assured of God's providential care for Ishmael and his mother, Abraham gave both of them a meager supply of bread and water, and sent them away toward "the Wilderness of Beersheba" (Gen. 21:14). Despite the fact that Ishmael was excluded from his earthly father's inheritance, due to Sarah's chronic prodding, his heavenly Father gave him and his descendants much more physical wealth than Abraham ever could have given him.

Moreover, the contributions of the Arabs to world civilization in practically every field of knowledge are immeasurable indeed. The contact with the Greek civilization gave the Arabs the opportunity to gradually develop their God-given intellectual genius and to establish their original mode of thought which was determined chiefly by their religious and philosophical views. Consequently, the world has benefited from the physical wealth and the intellectual contributions of the Arabs.

6

The Arab World

God promised not only to make of Ishmael "a great nation," but also to "bless him," and "make him fruitful," and "multiply him exceedingly," so that his descendants "shall not be counted for multitude" (Gen. 16:10; cf. 17:20).

History attests to the fact that this promise has been fulfilled with the evident rise and recent revival of Islam. Approximately 200 million Arabs are living today on more than 4 million square miles of land. The people who are called Arabs are the inhabitants of Lebanon, Syria, Jordan, Iraq, Yemen, Kuwait, Saudi Arabia, Egypt, Sudan, Palestine, Abu Dhabi, Oman, Dubai, Bahrain, Algeria, Qatar, Lybia, Morocco, Tunisia, and their offspring who live abroad. The majority of the Arabs are Muslims, though more than 1 billion Muslims in the world are not Arabs.

All that we know of ancient history down to the appearance of the Greeks took place in the region between the Nile Valley and Mesopotamia. The ancient countries in this region are mainly Arab lands.[1]

The Middle East possesses the most important strategic location on earth, which serves as the gateway to three continents: Asia, Europe, and Africa. God has also blessed the Arabs with "more than half the total proven oil reserves of the world. . . . Access to Arab oil is vital to the world's survival."[2]

The Western world must realize that ignorance about Arabian culture and history is not "bliss," but a detriment to international relations—especially when the West is striving feverishly to establish closer ties and a better understanding with the Arab world. Unfortunately, the picture that the Westerner has of the Arabs is misleading and usually stereotyped.

> The first images that come to the Westerner's mind when he thinks of the Arabs are sand, desert, camels, oil wells, irrational mobs . . . corrupt leadership, the Arabian Nights, harem, caliphs, passionate love, and the like.[3]

When I came from Lebanon in 1953 to pursue my education in music, my American college friends wanted to know, among other things, if I brought my camel with me. The funny thing about this is that they were gullibly serious. Even though I never rode a camel in Lebanon or anywhere else in the Middle East, I persuaded my curious friends to believe that when I discovered that I could not ride a camel on the U.S. highways, I traded my pet for a Volkswagen.

However, many inquisitive persons in recent times are surging out of North America into the Middle East and Spain in order to learn about the Arab world and its dominant role in history. These inquisitive persons are finding out, some of them for the very first time, that the Arabs are highly intelligent and personable and that they had ruled in Spain their vast empire for almost 800 years, from the seventh century until 1492, the year Christopher Columbus discovered America.

Westerners are learning with great interest that right after the death of prophet Muhammad in 632, the creed of Islam spread swiftly throughout the Middle East to North Africa, India, Central Asia, and Spain. Islam's call to prayer was heard from minarets embracing the Mediterranean, the Atlantic, and all the way to the outskirts of China—an empire much larger than Rome's at its zenith.

The Arabs were erroneously called "Moors" by Western historians. The word *Moor* is derived from Morocco. The Moors were Berbers who inhabited Morocco and were converted to Islam by the Arabs. The Muslims married into Visigoth and Spanish families, and also took for themselves fair-skinned Galatian wives. This kind of blood infusion of race and culture produced the exciting cultural legacy of Islamic Spain.

Much of the Spanish character, temperament, architecture, poetry, plant life, physical features and beauty, language, and music are blended from an Arabic and Muslim heritage.

The beauty of chaste Muslim women in Spain was a perennial source of inspiration to the great Arab poets and musicians. Muslim Spain enjoyed a degree of cultural achievement unequalled in the rest of Europe. Philosophy, music, poetry, literature, mathematics, theology, and medicine flourished. Scholars from around the world flocked to Spain and sat under the teachings of the Arabs, who in addition to their original encyclopedic works, translated and introduced the works of the Greeks, such as Euclid, Ptolemy, Plato, and Aristotle.

Arabic poetry inspired the first ballads of the European troubadors and influenced the songs of gypsy flamenco guitarists. To this day, flamenco singers and guitarists still entertain Spanish Muslims. Non-Muslim music lovers who are living in Spain also share the same love for the art of flamenco, especially when professional flamenco dancers perform under the fusillade of the guitarist's minor chords. These are just a few cultural contributions of the Muslims. I would like at this time to acquaint the reader with a brief background of some of the Arab countries.

Before completing the requirements for my doctor of philosophy degree in music education at Florida State University, I asked my major adviser if I could write my dissertation on the influence of the Arabs on Spanish music. I was told that since no one on the faculty knew practically anything about Arabic history and music, I should work on another project. I ended up writing a practical dissertation, entitled, "A Survey Appraisal of Music in the Schools of Lebanon." After earning a Ph.D. in 1967, I went back to Lebanon and pioneered by introducing instrumental music and music education in the public schools of Lebanon.

Lebanon

Lebanon is called "the Switzerland of the Middle East," but it is more than that. Before the recent civil war, Lebanon was a thriving democratic country experiencing an explosive economic boom, with one of the highest standards of living in the world and a literacy rate of more than 90 percent. It is a country steeped in culture and history with Roman ruins rivaling those in Greece and Rome. It is a land of biblical cities such as Sidon, Tyre, and Byblos. The word *Bible* is derived from Byblos, meaning papyrus or reed, used in ancient times for making scrolls and books.

It was in the vicinity of Tyre and Sidon where the Lord Jesus met the Syrophoenician woman. The term *Syrophoenician* refers to the people of Lebanon who were living in the proximity of Syria. The Lord tested her faith by referring to the haughty and unfounded claim of the unconverted Jews who believed that they were the chosen people of God and that the Gentiles were "dogs." This is what He said, "It is not good to take the children's bread and throw it to the little dogs." The woman replied with a broken and humble heart, "True, Lord, yet even the little dogs eat the crumbs which fall from their masters' table." The Lord marveled at her strong faith and said to her, "O woman, great is your faith! Let it be to you as you desire" (Matt. 15:26–28). The Lord delivered the woman's daughter from her vexation with a devil, and undoubtedly the woman and her daughter did receive the free gift of eternal salvation by faith in the Lord and Savior, Jesus Christ.

Lebanon is a small country in western Asia, also known as the Near East or the Middle East. It stretches along part of the eastern shores of the Mediterranean Sea. Being a central part of the Levant (the word *levant* derives its meaning from the word for the rising of the sun), Lebanon's role as a crossroads is continuous from the dawn of its history to the present. Its strategic position is not restricted to the traffic in people and goods, but also in international ideas for which Lebanon has been known to serve as a place for incubation.

Its area is approximately 4,000 square miles, and its population varies between two to three million inhabitants. It has two mountain ranges extending from its northern to southern borders. One parallels its seacoast, rising majestically tall to a maximum elevation of about 11,000 feet, and the other lies in the background. The mountains intercept the westerly maritime winds and tap their rain resources. Average annual rainfall in Lebanon is about 40 inches. Precipitation is normally accounted for between December through February, and sometimes in March. The weather is semi-tropical. The average temperature of Beirut is about 70 degrees Fahrenheit. However, in villages and towns perched on mountainous tips, winters are fairly cold and summers cool. The main sources of income for Lebanon are agriculture, tourism, shipping, and banking. Before the civil war, Lebanon was the financial center of the Arab world.

Historically, Lebanon was first inhabited by the Canaan- ites, around 3000 B.C., the same kind of people who occu- pied the rest of the Levantine strip in western Asia during the centuries between the two old civilizations of Mesopota- mia and Egypt. The Canaanites in Lebanon were called "Phoenicians" by the Greeks, after the purple-dyed textile they traded with them. "The purple dye was derived from shellfish in the waters of Lebanon's seashore, the throat of each shellfish producing only one drop of the dye. The purple-garment industry was very costly due to the pains- taking procedure of extracting the dye from the shellfish. The Phoenicians trimmed their textile products with it and wove it into their rugs and tapestries."[4]

Besides their carrying on trade and forming commercial stations everywhere their vessels took them, the Phoenicians derived their great wealth from their manufacturing. The chief product of their textile fabrics was a famous dye, ob- tained in minute drops from a shellfish, called the buccinum or the murex. This purple dye was of a dark red-violet, giv- ing various shades. Silk, cotton, and linen fabrics were dyed with beautiful results, but the most exquisite effects were obtained from woolen goods. The costly dye was employed only for materials of the best quality.

The country of Phoenicia was exceedingly fertile, being abundantly watered. The coast abounded with good har- bors, and the cedars of Lebanon furnished material in great quantities for shipbuilding. The most important and re- nowned cities on the coast were Tyre and Sidon. Beirut, the capital of Lebanon, is sixteen miles north of Sidon, and the principal seaport of Phoenicia.

The Phoenicians were a branch of the Semitic race through intermarriage with the Hebrews, the Arabs, the Syrians, the Assyrians, and later the Babylonians. Originally the Phoenicians were considered as the Canaanites of the coast and descendants of Canaan, the youngest son of Ham (Gen. 10:6). The Phoenicians migrated from the plains of Chaldaea soon after the death of Nimrod. They were never able to unite under one government. Each Phoenician city with its adjacent territory constituted a small independent state with a hereditary sovereign at its head. On the other hand, the Phoenicians would unite in a confederacy in certain emergencies, only when a common danger threatened the existence of the country, or when a common interest demanded unity.

Phoenicia (Lebanon) was, and still is, a prey to all conquerors who covet its strategic geographical location and its sources of wealth and natural beauty. For these reasons Phoenicia's independence has always been of short duration, and only sporadically were these renowned commercial peoples free from the yoke of foreign exploiters. These absorbing facts may shed some light on the recent turmoil in Lebanon.

Sidon, the oldest son of Canaan (Gen. 10:15), was the name of the first Phoenician city, which became very wealthy and powerful. Sidon engaged in commercial enterprises with different nations by land and sea, and was the first to found colonies. Tyre was the first colony of Sidon. Around the eleventh century before the birth of Christ, Tyre became the leading city of Phoenicia in wealth and splendor. The biblical king of Tyre, Hiram, was a good friend of both monarchs, David and Solomon. Hiram entered into commercial alliances with the illustrious Hebrew kings. He furnished Solomon with cedars and other materials used in the construction of the Jewish Temple at Jerusalem. After the death of Hiram, King Eth-Baal (or Ithobalus) gave his daughter Jezebel in marriage to Ahab, king of Israel. Afterward, the Phoenicians came under the yoke of many conquerors: the Assyrians, the Babylonians, the

Medo-Persians, the Greeks, the Romans, the Ottoman Turks, and others.

The Phoenicians extended their trade by establishing colonies and trading stations in many distant lands. For instance, the island of Cyprus, called Kittim or Chittim in Scripture (Gen. 10:4), was a colony of the Tyrians. Sicily and Sardinia became naval stations for Phoenician vessels employed in the trade with Western Europe, especially with Spain, called Tarshish in Scripture (Gen. 10:4). The Phoenicians established on the Mediterranean the colonies of Malaca (modern Malaga), the Straits of Gibraltar, and Tartessus (modern Cadiz). From Tartessus and Gades, the Phoenicians went to England in a search for tin, to Africa for apes, and to the coasts of the North Sea and the Baltic for amber.

The Phoenicians gave the Western world its alphabet. They were also known for commerce, and wherever their trade carried them they settled. Around 1000 B.C., they founded Gades, a town on the southern rocky tip of Spain, later known as Gibraltar. The Strait of Gibraltar separates the tip of Spain from Africa by about nine miles. Gibraltar derives from the Arabic *jabal Tariq*, meaning Tariq's mountain. Gibraltar was named after Tariq ibn Ziyad, who set sail with his Muslim army to conquer Spain. He landed at what is now called the Rock of Gibraltar around A.D. 711.

The Phoenicians also sailed the Atlantic Ocean to England in search of tin and other materials. Of all their colonies, the one that made its mark in history was Carthage. Planted around 800 B.C. in what is today Tunisia, Carthage developed into an empire that embraced North Africa and southern Spain. Carthaginian general Hannibal (247–183 B.C.) contested supremacy of the Mediterranean with emerging Rome and came near to achieving it.[5]

When under Alexander the Great (356–323 B.C.), western Asia, along with Egypt, Persia, and Mesopotamia, were swept by the Greek conqueror, then thirty-three years of age. Lebanon was included under the new rule. The fusion of the Greek legacy with the ancient civilizations produced the Hellenistic culture. This was altered somewhat as the Romans took over western Asia and the rest of the Mediterranean contour.

In Lebanon, cities like Antioch, Baalbek, Tyre, Sidon, and Byblos bear to this day the mark of their Roman heritage. In the third decade of the seventh century, Roman rule was put to an end as the followers of prophet Muhammad swarmed out from the Arabian Peninsula to sweep the Fertile Crescent and later on to push east as far as the Indus River and west through North Africa to Spain, where they ruled their vast empire from the early eighth to the fifteenth century. What ended their rule and caused their defeat were not the Battle of Tours and of Poitiers, as the English and French historians tell us, but their defeat was caused from within.

Edward Gibbon and other Western historians contend that the Arabs were defeated at the Battle of Tours, when the armies of Abd-Al-Rahmān and Charles Martel met. In reality, the Battle of Tours decided nothing at all. Like the Romans and other world powers, the Arabs were defeated because of chronic internal discord and jealousy among the greedy leaders.

Intoxicated with their victories and wealth, the Muslims began to dispute among themselves and waste their wealth and talents on worldly pleasures. The decline and fall of every world power is caused by similar problems and addictions.

The Ottoman Turks appeared in history and inherited the rule of the Arabs from the middle of the sixteenth century until the advent of the First World War. In 1860, Mount Lebanon managed, with the help of the French, to cut for itself an autonomous status, by reason of its concentration of a

Catholic-Christian population. After the defeat of the Ottoman empire at the end of World War I in 1918, Lebanon became a mandated territory of the French government until 1943, when it acquired its independence.

I am so grateful to God for helping me to immigrate to America in 1953. Here I met the same Lord and Master of Abraham and Hagar, who also gave me eternal salvation and set me free from the shackles of nepotism and idolatry. Although I have been cured from idolizing my beloved native country, I still love Lebanon very much, and more often than not I pray with tears for the welfare of its inhabitants.

Lebanon's predicament is a universal problem. The majority of the world's population love their native countries more than God. They idolize their lands and other properties and are willing to die for them. This is called idolatry and God hates it. This does not mean that one should not defend his country in case of war. What God said to Lebanon in the following verse, should be heeded by all nations. "O inhabitant of Lebanon, making your nest in the cedars, how gracious will you be when pangs come upon you, like the pain of a woman in labor?" (Jer. 22:23).

I agree with those who believe that God created Lebanon as the most beautiful country. The Bible compares Lebanon with the Messiah's glorious return. "The glory of Lebanon shall be given to it. . . . They shall see the glory of the Lord, the excellency of our God" (Isa. 35:2). I am sure that the peace and beauty of Lebanon will be perfectly restored at the forthcoming return of the Prince of peace. Meanwhile, wise men and women should occupy themselves with God's business till He comes (Luke 19:13).

My reminiscences of Lebanon come to me frequently, especially when I am totally absorbed in solitary creative work, such as when I am laboring on a manuscript or listening actively to good music of different cultures and styles. I remember vividly the glorious beauty of Lebanon and the bittersweet experiences of my childhood upbringing. What I recollect most of all is the time when I used to take long strolls meanderingly along the seashores of Beirut, where miles of clean sandy beaches greet bathers and water skiers all the year round.

One somber winter day I found myself sitting pensively near a window in a restaurant by the sea, overlooking the uninterrupted, clamorous waves of the Mediterranean. The elusiveness of their continual noise gave me pause for thought. After gazing at the intricate movements of the waves, I began to contemplate the mystery of birth and death. At first, I could barely see the birth of the waves no matter how hard I tried to trace their inception with my naked eyes. Subsequently, the waves took shape and gradually started to rise, one after another in sequential motion, until they reached their ultimate height. Then, suddenly, they disappeared over the sandy shore of Ras-Beirut, never to be seen again.

Alphonse-Marie-Louis de Prat de Lamartine (1790–1869), a French poet and historian, visited Lebanon and was reported to have said as he watched the waves that each wave was born so it can die in order to make room for the next wave that follows it. There is a parallel here between the birth and death of the waves and that of human life.

I was a teenager then and an aspiring dramatic actor and singer. My aspiration caused much grief and humiliation to my prideful aristocratic family. My father was appointed by the French government as a prosecutor general at Hawran (biblical Haran), a southwestern subregion of Syria, during the late 1920s. My grandfather was the spiritual head of the Druze religion in Lebanon. The Druze religion is an offshoot of the Shiite Muslim sect. The Druze people "have their roots in a splinter group from the Ismaili branch of Islam, which founded the Fatimid Caliphate of Egypt in the tenth century."[6] I discovered my acting and musical talents after the untimely death of my parents when I was in my teens.

My aristocratic upbringing discouraged manual labor and catered to my every wish and whim. It frowned upon any profession that is sought by a commoner or is related to the entertainment field. Nevertheless, the untimely death of my parents in the late 1930s changed my life-style abruptly. I was seven years old when my father was murdered by his political enemies in Syria, and about eleven years old when my mother was murdered by distant relatives, who collaborated with an American physician for the love of money.

To top it all off, all my inheritance was usurped, I was uprooted from my beloved country in 1953, and my umbilical cord was severed from the relatives and friends of my youth when I was converted to Christianity in 1955. I am happy to say at this time that "I also count all things loss for the excellence of the knowledge of Christ Jesus my Lord, for whom I have suffered the loss of all things, and count them as rubbish . . . that I may know Him and the power of His resurrection, and the fellowship of His sufferings, being conformed to His death" (Phil 3:8–10).

Before the Lord gave me love for my enemies, I was determined to obey the law of blood revenge as I was conditioned to believe: "eye for eye, tooth for tooth" (Lev. 24:20). No one can be persuaded to love his enemies without the regenerating power of the Holy Spirit. The Lord Jesus said, "Love your enemies, bless those who curse you, do good to those who hate you, and pray for those who spitefully use you and persecute you" (Matt. 5:44). This is true Christianity put in action, but those who are practicing such a miraculous transformation are hard to find.

Lebanon comes from the Arabic word *leben* or *laban*, meaning yogurt. When the high mountain ranges are covered in snow, the white waves resemble yogurt. One can see the mountains from Beirut, which look different every day due to the changing light from the clouds and the clear blue sea. No one who has visited Lebanon could honestly say that the universe was not created by God.

Living in Beirut kept me in balance, a highly complex balance of all elements of life: physical, spiritual, mental, and social. Beirut prepared me to face the future with courage and perseverance. I soon learned to carve for myself a thriving career of singing. I made many friends from all walks of life. I composed beautiful music and sang on the radio and in picnics up on high places, where the aromas in those spicy hills permeated the air. The fact that I had so much outdoor physical happiness was the perfect therapy for my lingering emotional suffering.

Egypt

After the untimely death of my parents, I became enamored with singing and composing Arabic music. Music gave me much solace and kept me from the strong temptation of being infected with destructive habits. At the age of eighteen, I succeeded in winning a singing competition and began a thriving career as a singer on the major Lebanese radio station in Beirut. Soon enough, I became a well-known singer and was able to accumulate a small fortune. Thereafter, I was encouraged by many friends across the Middle East to pursue my musical future in Egypt, because Cairo was the mecca of the Arabian artists and the Hollywood of the Near East.

In 1949 I flew to Cairo with my little fortune and big dreams of becoming a famous singer and movie actor. Little did I know that a new kind of suffering and deprivation would take place in my young life.

Egypt, like any other country, is saturated with good and

evil. An international charismatic swindler had no difficulty persuading me, by using indirect psychology, to give him all of my savings. This I did willingly and gullibly with the belief that I was saving his life from a man who wanted the exact amount that I gave away. The man disappeared from my life, leaving me mercilessly penniless. What transpired after that moment cannot be explained adequately.

The exciting thing about such a predicament is that God allowed me to experience different kinds of suffering and deprivation, even long before I was called to His service, so that I would be able to minister to people from all walks of life. I can attest to the fact that the Lord has rescued me several times by turning the evil that was meant against me into a great blessing—much the same as Hagar and Ishmael experienced.

I am very happy to say that my academic and vocational training in Lebanon and Egypt, coupled with the experiences of life, have been a great help in the writing of this book. In addition to the memory of my unforgettable youthful experiences, I kept a good diary of the things that I have learned in the various schools.

During my journey to Egypt in 1949–1952, I was fascinated with the historical sites. The early Egyptians had great talents in art and science; architecture was the greatest of all their arts. The buildings had distinguishing features of massiveness and grandeur, and are adorned with elaborately sculptured colossal statues. The beauty of their masonry has never been surpassed.

Egypt may not be the oldest nation, but its history is the oldest known to man. The ruins and monuments of ancient civilization found in the Nile Valley make Egypt's gigantic architectural works the most interesting as well as the most ancient in the world. Egypt is the birthplace of art and science.

I visited Memphis and saw the splendid pyramids, which

extend for about seventy miles on the west bank of the Nile, and among which are the popular Pyramids of Giza. The pyramids were all built on strictly scientific and mathematical principles. There was also the Great Sphinx (woman-headed lion), 146 feet long and 30 feet wide across the shoulders. Here are found the villages of Karnak and Luxor, great palaces, huge statues, tombs of kings and queens hewn in solid rock, and many more interesting findings.

Egypt was the ancient world's university, where Moses, Plato, Pythagoras, and other philosophers and historians were students. The discovery of the famous Rosetta Stone in 1799 led to the deciphering of the hieroglyphic inscriptions on the monuments, which were unknown to the Greeks and other ancient nations. The Rosetta Stone is now in the British Museum.

The Egyptians made so many significant contributions to civilization that it would not be possible to mention them all at this time. They were the first people to lay the foundation for an organized system of ancient warfare. The war-chariots formed the most important part of the Egyptian army. These chariots were drawn by two horses and usually contained two warriors—one to manage the horses, the other to fight. The national weapon was the bow, and the Egyptians were the most skilled archers of antiquity—a practice inherited from the days of Ishmael (Gen. 21:20).

No country in the world has so rich a heritage of monuments and other historical contributions as Egypt. From the land of the pharaohs came the stimulus for numerous intellectual achievements of later centuries. Important elements of science, architecture, philosophy, mathematics, literature, theology, and art flourished there. These Egyptians developed one of the oldest systems of political theory and jurisprudence. They also originated architectural principles that were destined to be used by subsequent generations.

Since the time of Plato, the intellects and artists traveled to Egypt to marvel at its cultural institutions and storehouse of antiquities. The oldest architectural wonders are the three famous pyramids of Giza and the temples at Karnak and Luxor, which were built between 2780–2270 B.C. The main significance of the pyramids was religious and political. Their construction was an attempt to guarantee immortality for the pharaohs and to endow the state with permanence.

The temples surpass the pyramids in architectural form and splendor, and are characterized by massive size. The Karnak temple is the largest religious edifice ever built. Its central hall alone could contain almost any of the big Gothic cathedrals of Europe.

Aramco World Magazine allowed me to ferret out its printed materials related to some of the topics under discussion in this chapter. In the July-August 1987 issue, there was an article written by John Lawton concerning the performance of Guiseppe Verdi's *Aida* at Luxor.

Aida is the most popular of Verdi's operas. It was written at the request of the Viceroy of Egypt, Khedive Ismail, who had built a sumptuous opera house in Caira for *Aida*, which was first performed there on December 24, 1871. However, *Aida*'s recent performance at Luxor Temple's inner sanctum, coupled with the haunting production of Western talents, against the stunning natural beauty of the Sphinx overlooking the Nile River, not only positively mesmerized the audience, but also stirred up my imagination and rekindled my love for the opera and brought back some unforgettable memories of my artistic days in Egypt.

After having established a name for myself in Lebanon as a singer-composer, I set out for the mecca of the Arabian artists in 1949. Cairo was then the Hollywood of the Middle East, and the hub of the Egyptian aristocracy and European elite who led a life of profuse extravagance. Cairo was truly cosmopolitan during the time of King Farouk, when Muslims, Christians, Jews, and others lived in a multi-cultural environment. (I do not know what Cairo is like today. I left Egypt when King Farouk was dethroned and deported in 1952, after I managed to participate in a movie.)

I have found the Egyptians to be gracious and kind with an unmatched sense of humor. Cairo reminded me of the undisciplined drivers of Beirut when it comes to traffic regulations and the keeping of appointments. These characteristics are not restricted to cabdrivers only. More than seventy-five years ago, T. E. Lawrence spoke to this effect, saying: "The Semitic mind does not lean toward a system of organization. It is practically impossible to fuse the diverse elements among the Semites into a modern, closely knit state."

Cabdrivers rarely pay any attention to policemen who stand frantically directing the traffic jams with their whistles and waving of the arms. Speed limits are usually not enforced, and whoever has the largest vehicle and honks loudest has the right of way. With all of this seeming disorganization, drivers in Cairo and Beirut have a lower rate of accidents than in the West.

I have not seen anywhere a more unquenchable optimism than that of the Egyptians. No matter how bad things were, the Egyptians were able to joke about their problems and anything else, but never about their religion. I was really impressed by their faith and knowledge of the Qur'an. The more I heard them recite the Qur'an, the more I fell in love with the teachings of Muhammad, and I was almost persuaded to become one of his followers, particularly when I began to visit Al-Azhar.

Al-Azhar, meaning "The Resplendent," is the world's oldest and most important university of Islam. According to the Muslim lunar calendar, al-Azhar's millennium celebrations did take place in 1942. For more than a thousand years the people in Cairo have been called to prayer five times a day from the minaret of the al-Azhar's mosque. In the morning they are awakened by the beautiful voice of the *muezzin* crying, "Allah is Great, and Muhammad is His messenger." Many pray in their homes kneeling on rugs or mats, or wherever they may be at the time the call to prayer is announced. Others go to the mosque of al-Azhar, slipping off their shoes or sandals as they enter through the gate. Artisans in stained kaftans, students and clerks in trousers and jackets with or without flowing robes become quietly respectful as they cross the sunny courtyard to the sanctuary.

Inside the sanctuary, professors in gray kaftans and red felt caps wound with a broad white linen band spend much time lecturing to their students. The students sit on great red carpets cross-legged. For more than a thousand years students have clustered round the pillars of al-Azhar to learn theology and Muslim law in perfect Arabic and to memorize the Qur'an. The science of memory work is the basis of the curriculum in higher education. The retentive faculties are developed by stressing memory work. I was told by a sheikh in al-Azhar that al-Ghazzāli earned a title, the authority of Islam, by memorizing 300,000 traditions, and Ahmad ibn-Hanbal memorized one million traditions. Poets were known for their memory work. Having read a copy of a book, the renowned poet al-Mutanabi' saw no more need for buying the book, because he already stored its contents in his mind. Arab scholars had prodigious memories because they were trained from childhood to memorize, and this tradition has been passed on to their posterity.

The influence of al-Azhar extends far beyond Egypt. To the vast Muslim world, al-Azhar is comparable to Oxford University and to the best seminaries and houses of parliament in the Western world. It is the nodal center of Muslim faith with its own synod of sheikhs who study and define secular law based on the teachings of prophet Muhammad. Makkah is the heart of Islam, but al-Azhar is its head. The Rector or Sheikh of al-Azhar hands down both religious and secular decisions to Muslim jurists and theologians.

There was always something interesting to do in Cairo. One day a Muslim friend took me to see how the ancient craft of making huge tent pavillions is carried on. We went together to the tenth-century gate of Bab Zuwayla in old Cairo, and I witnessed for the first time the dazzling art of tentmaking. The ancient craft of this amazing art has been passed on from father to son for hundreds of years.

There is more to tentmaking than at first meets the eye. All of the designs used in the making of a tent must first be drawn on large sheets of brown paper. A fine needle point pricks out the outline of each pattern in thousands of small holes. The perforated sheet of paper is then laid upon each piece of colored cloth—usually in brilliant red, blue, yellow, or scintillating green. A black carbon dust is sprinkled over the paper so that the dust percolates through the holes, leaving behind a fine stencil outline of the pattern pounced onto the cloth, ready to be cut out. This is one of the many painstaking processes which is done in order to produce one tent.

I was told that more than a thousand years ago, the Fatimid rulers of Egypt used huge tents made with gold brocade and silk supported by silver poles. One of the caliph's tents required 100 camels to transport and had taken fifty artists nine years to make. Today, on the prophet Muhammad's birthday, a spacious tent pavillion rises not far from the University of al-Azhar. Religious, groups from all over Egypt come to Cairo to celebrate.

Cairo is the largest city in Africa. It is the intellectual, religious and educational center of the Arab world, the Hollywood of the Middle East, the seat of journalism and book publishing. With all its ills, Cairo is still the most interesting city in the Middle East and Africa.

I used to study my Qur'an on the balcony of my apartment in the blissful still of early morning, when Cairo was bathed in the clear blue of desert dawn. I remember vividly seeing the visible evidence of a city that was once among the most important on earth. Unlike the barren Arab cities built by petrodollars, Cairo had substance and soul. Its open-air cafés throbbed with life, and its noisy streets were crowded with people and vehicles until the wee hours of the morning. In many ways, Cairo was an emotional magnet vibrating with excitement, a city where an Arab may very well feel at home.

Al-Qahira is the Arabic word for Cairo, meaning the tormentor. The term is used to portray a platonic relationship between a man and a woman. One may dislike and be tormented with the filth, congestion, and nerve-racking noise of Cairo, but the person would surely experience a unique love affair with this wondrous city.

I was told that Plato studied for a short time in Cairo and marveled at the three Great Pyramids of Giza, and that the French elite in Cairo still speak of the legacy of Napoleon Bonaparte's scientific expedition to Egypt some two centuries ago. The beautiful architecture of the Romanesque, the French, the domes of the Mamluks, and of other cultures—all of these historical facts ought to remind us that Cairo was and remains a juxtaposition of old and new, where East and West took part in the shaping of Cairo's amiable character.

The Suez Canal was built by the Frenchman Ferdinand-marie de Lesseps, and it opened in 1869 as a gateway to three continents: Africa, Asia, and Europe. Since that time, cotton became king, and life was a lavish extravagance for the elite of Europe and the Middle East and others, until the deportation of King Farouk in 1952. When I came to Egypt in 1949 to pursue my aspiration in singing and acting, I used to sit on my balcony and see the minarets of several tall and graceful mosques that dwarfed everything in sight. My apartment was on the second floor of an old but nice building overlooking the smooth waters of the Nile River. Daily before sunrise the beautiful voices of the muezzins summoned the faithful Muslims to prayer.

Cairo was truly cosmopolitan. Muslims, Christians, Jews, and other nationalities and races lived together in peace and were able to communicate with each other amicably. God has created a wonderful world and enough land for the human race to live in peace. I am praying that the Arabs and Jews and others will become friends again and be able to co-exist in peace, with the help of God!

United Arab Emirates

The United Arab Emirates comprise seven federated states: Abu Dhabi, Dubai, Sharjah, Ajman, Um al-Quaiwain, Ras al-Khaimah, and Fujairah. With the discovery of oil wells in 1959, the barren lands of the coastal towns of the Arabian Gulf have channeled their petroleum wealth toward the building of a modern society: schools, hospitals, banks, luxurious hotels, beautiful harbors, factories, farms, and sturdy highways that rarely need any repair from year to year. The seven states obtained their total independence from Great Britain in 1971 and became known as the United Arab Emirates.

The most important neighbor of these states is the independent country of Oman, mainly because it commands the western shores of the strategic Strait of Hormuz—gateway to Arabian Gulf Oil, and also because it was the ancient world's chief supplier of copper and frankincense. The country of Oman was isolated from the neighboring seven states and was plagued by poverty until the discovery of oil in 1964.

It is interesting to note that some archaeologists have discovered recently that the mysterious country of "Makan" or "Magan" mentioned in Sumerian tablets has been traced to modern Oman. Ancient Oman had a flourishing copper ore mining and processing industry. More than 3,000 years ago, miners from "Magan" dug and processed tons of copper ore and exported it via "Dilmun," modern Bahrain, to Sumer (see *Aramco World Magazine*, March-April 1980). Sumerian inscriptions on tablets found in modern Iraq clearly confirm this information.

Dhofar, now part of Oman, was also the source of frankincense, offered by the Queen of Sheba to King Solomon and by the Magi to the infant Jesus. The Magi were actually very important rulers of Arab tribes who had a large entourage of loyal fighting men who obviously served as their bodyguards. The Magi were more than three wise men, and they were interested in the birth of Christ probably because they were descendants of Abraham through Hagar and Keturah. They knew the prophecies concerning the "Coming One" who was to sit on David's throne in Jerusalem. Tertullian (A.D. 160–230) said that the Magi were Arabs. According to the understanding of the early church fathers, the gifts that the Magi gave to the Lord Jesus had symbolic meaning. Gold symbolized Christ's deity, frankincense symbolized His purity, and myrrh symbolized His death, since it was used for embalming.

Arab products and contributions are understood from ancient tradition, though for the most part they are undocumented. God has bestowed upon the Arabs many blessings (Gen. 17:20), and these blessings have been exported and shared with the rest of the world. For thousands of years gold, frankincense, and myrrh were symbols of great wealth and luxury for the mightiest civilizations. The highest tribute anyone could give to a king at that time, as the Arab Magi gave to the Lord Jesus, was to offer Him nature's most precious products. When the Queen of Sheba gave King Solomon such products (1 Kings 10:10), she came to seek his wisdom "out of the wilderness like pillars of smoke, perfumed with myrrh and frankincense" (Song 3:6).

These precious natural resources, like petroleum today, were the basis of a number of popular commodities which brought great wealth during the Greek and Roman periods. In the centuries that followed, the Arabs developed a more scientific approach to the creation of perfumes, adding the fragrances of a variety of flowers to the traditional aromatic woods. During the reign of the Umayyad and Abbassid caliphs, when the Arabs ruled a vast empire stretching from India to Spain, chemists created a floral essence, called *itr* in Arabic, that is still called by its Arabic name: attar of roses. Many other creations of perfumes were brought back by the Crusaders from their wars in the Middle East. These perfumes revolutionized Europe's ideas of cosmetics, which until the Middle Ages had been restricted to paints. Eventually the skills of perfume production were transmitted from Arab Spain to other parts of the earth.

The resin of the frankincense tree, *Boswellia sacra*, is collected in two-handled baskets by shaving ovals of bark with a putty knife, called *minqaf*, and from these wounds the resin oozes out and hardens into tear-like droplets, which are scraped off the tree and put in the baskets. Oman's Dhofar province and Hadramawt have always been the cradle of all the varieties of frankincense craftsmanship. These trees still flourish today on the desert plateau of Arabia, nourished by the steady tropical sun and the heavy dew, unique to that part of the world. The pungent and pleasurable smell given off when frankincense is burned was and still is highly esteemed by the peoples of the Middle East and others; and the heady and allusive scent of this precious perfume is already making waves in many of the world's most exclusive stores.

Iraq

Recent archaeological excavations and reconstructions have provided us with remarkably accurate information of what Babylon must have been like under Nebuchadnezzar. The city of Babylon was located on both sides of the Euphrates, with fortified high walls, lofty temples, and magnificent palaces. Both sides of the city were connected by a stone bridge, the first ever known. It was built on a square pattern, and the streets were wide enough for two chariots drawn by four horses to pass each other.

The royal palace dominated one end of the city and was lavishly decorated, enamelled in brilliant brick relief, possessing several arches and vaulted stone structures. The famed Hanging Gardens of Babylon were built by Nebuchadnezzar for his wife, Amytas, so that she would not miss her mountain home. The gardens were kept green by an irrigation water supply system. This masterwork of engineering had its continuous water supply pumped from a well with a triple shaft to irrigate the varieties of trees and plants.

The other end of the city contained the Tower of Babel. The temple was built of blue enamelled bricks "to rival heaven", and its uppermost structure contained a twenty-foot-high seated statue of the god Marduk. The temple itself was square and consisted of eight towers, one resting on the other, and all resting upon a ziggurat. The top of the ziggurat was reached by a spiral staircase encircling the outside with seats halfway up for those who became tired as they climbed.[7]

The abundance of Iraq's present-day oil deposits has perhaps blurred the fact that it is "the Cradle of Civilization." It was there where the Garden of Eden was located; as were the home of the patriarch Abraham, the Tower of Babel, and the Hanging Gardens of Babylon. Jonah's tomb is located in the Iraqi city of Nebi Yunus, where it is visited frequently by Christians, Muslims, and Jews alike. It was also during the time of the Babylonian era that Hammurabi introduced his code of laws, which remained unsurpassed until the era of the Roman Empire. The use of the first wheel, mathematics, pictographic writing, the first written laws, and the plough took place in the Tigris-Euphrates Valley.[8]

Iraq survived the passing of many empires and cultures. Sumerians, Babylonians, Assyrians, Persians, Greeks, Romans, Arabs, Ottomans, and British—all contributed to Iraq's splendid history. Baghdad was the center of the Arab's Golden Age during the period of the Abbassid Caliphate (A.D. 750–1258). It was an era of splendor and magnificence. During that period Arabic numbers and the decimal system were introduced, as were algebra and many other literary and scientific works. Ambassadors were exchanged with other countries, and delegates were sent as far as India and China to establish commerce and trade relations. Baghdad was an open market for merchants from all over, and the traders ventured by land and sea. Iraqis and other Arabs sailed to China for silk and porcelain, to India for gold and spices, and to Zanzibar for ivory.

Today Iraq stands on the threshold of both the old and the new. The home of the great caliph, Harun al-Rashid, Baghdad reflects the country's affluence with its modern hotels, office buildings, banks, and many other attractions. At the same time, the capital city of Iraq still has the narrow twisting alleyways with its bazaars which were built during the Middle Ages, and even before that time.

Syria

Syria has an area of about 72,000 square miles. It is bounded by Lebanon and the Mediterranean Sea on the west, by Turkey on the north, by Iraq on the east, and by Jordan and Israel on the south. The Greeks regarded Syria as including Palestine and Phoenicia, but the Jews have always considered these three countries distinct from each other, until 1948, when Palestine was wrested by the Jews and became known as Israel.

Aram, one of the five sons of Shem, founded Syria. One of the chief mountains of Syria is Mount Lebanon, whose summit is said to be perpetually capped with snow. Damascus is the capital of Syria and it is believed that al-Sham, as the Arabs prefer to call it, is the most ancient city in the world. Antioch, the capital of Syria during the era of the Greek Empire, was celebrated for its beauty and magnificence. It was in this Syrian city that "the disciples were first called Christians" (Acts 11:26). There was another city in Asia Minor, called Antioch, also visited by the Apostle Paul (Acts 13:14). Other famous cities of ancient Syria were Tadmor, later became known as Palmyra, and the Greek Heliopolis (city of the sun), known as modern Baalbek in Lebanon.

The earliest inhabitants of Syria were the Aramaeans, who descended from Aram, Shem's youngest son (Gen. 10:22). Some of the posterity of Hamath is also said to have dwelt there in primitive times. Hamath is a son of Canaan (Gen. 10:18). The Hebrew Scriptures represent ancient Syria as divided into a number of small kingdoms, among which were Damascus, Hamath, Geshur, and Zobah. The Syrians were at first governed by numerous chiefs, called kings, a title which the ancient writers applied to every ruler or leader of a community.

During the period of Assyrian supremacy (dominated the ancient biblical world from the ninth through the seventh century B.C.), Syria was divided into at least five leading states: the Northern Hittites, whose capital city was Carchemish, on the Euphrates River; the Patena, on the Lower Orontes River, whose capital was Kinalua; the Hamathites, on the Upper Orontes River, whose capital city was Hamath (modern Hamah); the Southern Hittites, in the region south of Hamath; and the Syrians of Damascus, whose capital city was Damascus.[9]

Until recent history, Syria went under the successive rule of the Assyrians, the Babylonians, the Medo-Persians, the Greco-Macedonians, the Romans, the Saracens, the Seljuk Turks, the Mongol Tartars, the Ottoman Turks (for at least four centuries), and the French. Syria acquired its full independence from France in 1946. Lebanon went under the same treatment Syria had experienced. If nothing else I have learned from history, I have learned that all conquerors are alike. For instance, when the French defeated the Turkish Empire and seized Lebanon and Syria in 1918, instead of giving the people a self-rule policy, France came to stay and ruled the two Arab countries. The British did the same thing in Palestine when they made some promises to the Palestinians they did not intend to keep.

The German philosopher Hegel, said it best: "We ask men to study history, but the only thing that men learn from the study of history is that men learn nothing from the study of history." Hegel's sophistry may be considered empirically correct, in that when a world power helps a weaker nation, it is usually for self-interest.

Conversely, Damascus played an incomparable role as the seat of the Arab Empire under the Islamic rule of the Umayyads, rivaling Baghdad and Muslim Spain. Damascus was then the undisputed cultural center of the world. Famous Syrians included al-Fārābi (872–950) and al-Mutanabbi' (915–965).

Al-Mutanabbi's elegant style in rhymed prose mesmerized his hearers and fired their zeal for executing his intentions and desires. The poet laureate al-Mutanabbi's ornate and bombastic style "with its flowery rhetoric and improbable metaphors renders him to the present day the most popular and most widely quoted poet in the Moslem world. An early authority calls his poetry 'the height of perfection.'"[10] Al-Mutanabbi' was the greatest poet of his age, and his name has been immortalized in Islamic history.

The medieval golden age of lyric poetry reached its zenith during the seventh to the tenth century. The poems emanated from themes of love, hospitality, wars, courage, and patriotism. Poetry gained much prestige under the Umayyad Caliphs, when al-Akhtal and al-Farazdaq wrote their lyric masterpieces (around 640–732). These and other great Arabian poets were able to immortalize the form of lyric poetry. The sound of words and the rhythm and harmony produced by the phonetic beauty of the Arabic language invited unrestrained emotional and intellectual response.

The rhythm, the rhyme, and the musicality of the poems were able to hypnotize the hearers and had a magical influence on them. "The beauty of man," declares an Arab proverb, "lies in the eloquence of his tongue." Another Arab proverb says, "Wisdom is comprised of three things: the brain of the Franks, the hands of the Chinese, and the tongue of the Arabs." And the three most basic attributes of "the perfect man, are: Eloquence in both prose and lyric poetry, archery, and horsemanship."

The Arabian poet was honored as a great hero, and in war and peace his tongue had the power to arouse a nation in the same manner as the tirade of a talented political orator. His poems were committed to memory, and sometimes they were delivered in an impromptu bravura performance, and transmitted from one generation to another.

Apart from being the orator and spokesman of his community, the poet was also the historian and scientist. He was versed in genealogy and familiar with history and with all kinds of subjects, and he had no difficulty in bridging historical gaps and filling vacancies. In this way he was able to succeed in giving a continuous record from Adam to Muhammad, and so forth.

Islam considers Arabic to be the most important living Semitic language, mainly because the Qur'an is written in Arabic, and more than one billion Arabs and Muslims speak and pray in Arabic. Literary or classical Arabic is still employed today as the medium of communication in written and spoken form. Colloquial Arabic, which is the medium of general conversation, differs considerably from the classical language. The classical language could be understood by many Arabs, but colloquial Arabic is understood only by people who speak the same dialect. One Arabic dialect differs from another primarily in the addition of suffixes and prefixes.

Grammatically, Arabic has that distinctive feature of Semitic languages, the triconsonantal root consisting of three consonants separated by two vowels. The vowels are shown by symbols below or above the consonants. Arabic is written from right to left, and its alphabet is comprised of twenty-eight consonants which evolved from the Aramaic writing. Arabs from all walks of life have an almost mystical love for their language due to its beauty and rhythm and peculiarities.

However, the crowning contribution of the Arabs to the world was in the field of philosophic thought. They translated and transmitted Greek philosophy to the West, adding their own encyclopedic contribution, especially in reconciling faith and reason, religion and science. Philosophy as developed by the Greeks and monotheism as evolved from the teachings of the Christian Bible had to be harmonized. To this end the medieval Muslim thinkers of Baghdad, Damascus, Andalusia, and Cordova have been credited historically in the reconciliation of these two currents of thought. This and other contributions of the Arabs were of great magnitude, considering their effect upon scientific and philosophic thought and upon other fields of knowledge. Sadly enough, if Arab literature is little known outside the Middle East, it may be because of what the British writer John Fowles once called the "Linguistics Iron Curtain" that keeps much of Arab culture and history hidden from the West.

7

Understanding the Arab Mind and Culture

It is my sincere hope that the following information will provide a cross-cultural guide for people who are interested in a clearer understanding of the thought patterns and social practices of the Arabs. To my knowledge, no other book has ever been written from a positive approach with the intention to emphasize that the life-style of the Arabs, the good and not the destructive ways of life, ought to be appreciated rather than criticized. Here are a few thought patterns and cultural practices of the Arabs.

Legacy of Cooking

It has been said that "some people live to eat and others eat to live." The Arabs do both and enjoy every minute of it. The Semitic Arabs and their counterparts attach a great value to the historical art of cooking, which was passed on from Mesopotamia (modern Iraq). According to ancient history, the land between the Tigris and Euphrates Rivers was apparently the birthplace of *haute cuisine* as well as a cradle of civilization. The Sumerian-Akkadian bilingual dictionary, recorded in cuneiform script on twenty-four stone tablets about 1900 B.C., lists many terms in the Mesopotamian language for over 800 different items of food and drink, including 20 different kinds of cheese, more than 100 varieties of soup and 300 types of bread—each with different ingredients, filling, shape, and size.

Other archaeological findings suggest that a long shopping list of Mesopotamian dishes would be at least twice as long. For example, stone bas-reliefs were discovered at Nineveh showing servants carrying choice delicacies to the royal table, among them grasshoppers *en brochette* and meat-filled intestine casings. The Mesopotamians presumably made and ate the world's first known sausage.[1]

Records of deliveries to the royal kitchens at Ur included ducks, suckling pigs, pigeons, lambs, and geese. Other records list many kinds of fresh and saltwater fish, the preferred kinds being those raised in the reservoirs which were part of Mesopotamia's intricate irrigation system. The cornerstone of the Mesopotamian diet appears to have included chick-peas, lentils, onions, leeks, shallots, garlic, lettuce, cucumber, apples, pears, grapes, figs, pistachios, dates, and pomegranates. Also a wide range of spices and herbs were used. No wonder those peoples were healthy and lived longer than today's world population.

Mesopotamia (modern Iraq) rose to great prominence and splendor during the Abbassid Caliphate, when Islam was the most powerful influence in the world, and Baghdad became the political and cultural capital in A.D. 762. The Arabs introduced great refinement in eating habits. A prosperous cosmopolitan ruling elite had emerged whose members lived in luxury. The banquets at the courts of the caliphs were proverbial for their lavishness and gregariousness; and cooking was transformed into an art which reached unsurpassed heights.

Arab generosity is rooted deeply in the public conduct, and it has become a matter of habit rather than ostentation. It is practiced so naturally that social relations are carried on in an atmosphere of ease and informality. Hospitality is a virtue which has extended from the tents of Shem to the dwellings of Abraham, and to the farthest outreaches of the Muslim world. It is still very rare to visit an Arab home, whether it be poor or rich, without being impressed by the courtesy and hospitality which are extended to the visitor. Arabian history and literature are full of tales of flamboyant generosity and stupendous prodigality. A reputation of being hospitable is very valuable to an Arab in that the poorest host will literally kill the last sheep he possesses in order to provide a banquet for his guest.

The Arabs brought to each country they had conquered different tastes of foods: olive oil from Syria, dates from Iraq, and coffee from Arabia. Crops such as rice, sugar, eggplants, and spinach spread throughout the Muslim world. During the Abbassid period, from the ninth to the twelfth century, the Arab world saw great marriages of cooking styles and refinements in eating habits. Every poet, artist, physician, prince, and others took an interest in eating. Writing on what to eat was abundant and very popular. The taste for spiced foods and sweet things became popular, and they were prepared by professional chefs.

Social Etiquette

A guest never enters an Arab home without being offered something to eat or drink, with the assumption that the guest will not accept the invitation the first time, no matter how much he or she desires refreshment. If someone comes to a home while food is being served, the people eating always offer to share their food with the guest, whether the person is a friend or stranger. Of course, the guest is expected to decline at least three times before finally accepting to eat and drink.

When I came to America in 1953, I was invited by a Christian family for lunch. That was on a Sunday morning, and I had no choice but to go with them to church. I was so hungry in church that I could hardly wait until the preacher ended his boring sermon. When we reached the house and food was put on the table, a prayer of thanksgiving was uttered, then I was told only once to start eating. I had to decline as I was trained to do. The problem with such an unpleasant situation was that my hosts did not understand my native customs. I had to leave their home very hungry and disappointed, and I never saw them again. After that experience I have learned not to wait to be told more than once.

According to traditional society, the Arabs were trained to sit on rugs and eat only with the right hand. Today, silverware may be used, depending upon the people who choose the modern or traditional ways of eating. It is considered impolite to point the soles of one's feet toward another or to stare at anyone else while eating. After the meal is served and everyone has had enough to eat, bitter or sweet coffee is offered. It is poured from a shiny brass coffeepot held in the host's left hand into the small cups in his right hand, enough to give the drinker three to five sips. The cup is refilled several times until the guest signals he has had enough.

The making and offering of coffee is an important duty of a host, whether city-dweller, villager, or nomad. Great ceremony is given to coffee-making in the Arabian desert. The coffee beans are roasted over an open fire and pounded with a mortar. The coffee is then flavored with cardamom and served in tiny cups with no handles. Today in the city, coffee is made on the stove. I make my own coffee almost every morning and drink it with my wife.

The Arabs are gregarious and enjoy having people come to their homes often for meals and discussions. Invitations to meals are usually verbal and spontaneous. Meals in the West are served on time whenever an invitation takes place, but in the Middle East the Arabs love to invite people often to discuss various issues before the food is served. The Arabs have their favorite "hospitality stories" which they love to share with their guests before, during, and after the meal. They usually speak of their glorious and interesting past history, present world situation, and fatalistically relegate the future to the will of Allah.

Beliefs and Logic

When an American Christian missionary visits an Arab home in the Middle East, with the intention to share the love of Christ for the Arabs, the educated Muslim who is well versed in the Bible and the Qur'an loses no time in pointing out that Caleb, the Edomite, descended from people usually associated with the Arabs through intermarriage. Caleb was proselytized into the tribe of Judah, from which was born our Lord and Savior Jesus Christ (Num. 13:6); and that Moses married an Arab woman named Zipporah (Ex. 2:21); and that Joseph married Asenath, the daughter of an Egyptian priest (Gen. 41:45); and that the Arab tribe of Rechab was given a place of honor in the worship of Jehovah, and became an example of faithfulness to the tribe of Judah in Jerusalem (Jer. 35); and that the patriarch Job was an Arab, and the "wise men from the East" (Matt. 2:1), who followed the star to Jerusalem were also Arabs coming from North Arabia, "rather than Magi from Persia"[2] and so forth.

The Arabs place great value on piety, and Islam affects

their total way of life on a daily basis. They do believe in the virgin birth of Christ, and they feverishly study comparative religion so that the Muslim scholars will be able to persuade Christians who are interested in a debate with them that Islam is the final and inerrant revelation of God through Muhammad. This is the reason I discourage my students, and any Christian scholar, to seek a debate with Muslims, mainly because no one has ever been able to logically convince a Muslim to believe in the deity of Christ and the Trinity.

In comparing Christianity with Islam, the Muslim scholar tries to convince his hearers that his beliefs are based on logic and are more practical than those related to Christianity. To substantiate his argument, he appeals to the Qur'an by summarizing the basic tenets of his religious duties under the following pillars.

Shahādah, profession of faith.

To believe in Allah is not enough. The Muslim must make a public oral profession. The act of professing the belief that God is One God and Muhammad is His prophet constitutes the first pillar of Islam. The recitation of this declaration with genuine intention in the presence of at least two witnesses is sufficient for a person to become a Muslim.

Salāt, prescribed prayers.

Prayers must be offered five times daily, publicly or privately—at dawn, midday, mid-afternoon, sunset, and two hours after sunset. The Muslims are not ashamed of their God, and their "prayer call" is broadcast from the minaret of a mosque. They all pray facing in the direction of Makkah (Mecca). Prayer is regulated by ritual purification beforehand, somewhat similar to Old Testament practice, and a predetermined number of prostrations and genuflections while recitation is taking place.

Ironically, the Lord Jesus Christ commanded His followers

to "preach on the housetops" the gospel of eternal salvation (Matt. 10:27); and while the silent majority of the Christian world are dispelled by slumbering, the Muslims are preaching Muhammad's message "on the housetops," and they are having a world revival.

Zakāt, giving alms.

Muslims are required to give alms to the poor and needy, at least one-fortieth or 2.5 percent of their income. It is not uncommon to see beggars on the streets and near the mosques in Muslim countries. In addition to the giving of alms to the needy, billions of petro-dollars and monies from other incomes are being spent on building mosques around the world in order to propagate Islam. One Muslim friend told me recently that the reason God gave the Arabs much oil is because He wants the whole world to hear the message of Islam.

Everywhere I go to teach and speak on understanding Islam, I am usually asked to explain the rapid growth of Islam. I believe that the reason for Islam's popularity around the world is because the Muslims are taking their religion and calling very seriously. So instead of criticizing them for obeying the message of their prophet, why not try to emulate their zeal and determination to do likewise for our Lord and Savior, Jesus Christ!

Sawm, fasting.

Fasting is restricted to the ninth lunar month of Ramadan, the month when the Qur'an was revealed to Muhammad. "The Muslim calendar is based on twelve lunar months, and therefore it is approximately eleven days shorter than the solar year. In other words, Ramadan falls a bit earlier each year, and goes full cycle through the Gregorian (Western) calendar about every thirty-three years."[3]

The purpose of Ramadan is to experience hunger and

practice self-denial to the pleasures of life, and to bring with it a holiday atmosphere, when family and friends gather together to socialize and feast on elaborate meals.

Hajj, pilgrimage.

For nearly fourteen centuries the Hajj has been one of the most extraordinary religious gatherings in the world. Millions of Muslims have gathered in Saudi Arabia to celebrate the pilgrimage at Makkah. The Muslims, male and female, come from every corner of the earth to the holiest city of Islam. There are three holy cities of Islam, the other two are Medina and Jerusalem. The Hajj must be made between the eighth and the thirteenth days of the twelfth month of the Muslim lunar year.

Some of the most exciting features of the pilgrimage are the sacred mosque and the Kaabah with its silver framed Black Stone embedded in one wall, and covered by a black cloth with Qur'anic verses in gold. The Muslims kiss or touch the Black Stone, smoothed from millions of hands and lips, with the belief that it was a precious jewel brought out from Paradise by Adam, and later it was given to Ishmael by the angel Gabriel.

However, kissing or touching the Black Stone is only a ritual that is performed because Muhammad did it and not because it has any spiritual power.[4]

Jihad, to struggle for a holy cause.

According to Muslim belief, all healthy men, and occasionally women, must bear arms in the event of a holy cause that may or may not lead to war. Death in *jihad* is martyrdom. A warrior who gives his or her life for a holy cause will secure a beautiful place in paradise with special heavenly privileges. This is a good reason for foreign powers not to provoke the Muslims to wrath. Islam owes much of its popularity as a major world religion to this tenet.

Children's Education

In the traditional Arab family the children were educated at home as soon as they were able to talk. The father's duty was to teach them about God, and by the age of six, the child was held responsible to recite the ritual prayer. The Qur'an was used as a reading textbook in the elementary school. In addition to reading and writing, the students were taught Arabic grammar, history, poetry, arithmetic, and stories about Muhammad the prophet. They were also trained to use the bow and arrow and swim. The value of swimming was enhanced by life on the Mediterranean coast.

The ethical ideas of education as gleaned from Arabian literature on the subjects that were taught, were to train the students in courage, endurance in time of trouble, patience when tested, observance of the rights and obligations to neighbors, generosity, hospitality, manliness, courtesy, compassion for the needy, regard for women and fulfillment of solemn promises. These are recognized as the virtues highly prized in an Arab gentleman.

Memory work was emphasized throughout the child's education. Young students were encouraged to memorize the Qur'an, and they were trained to respect and honor their teachers. When a teacher entered a classroom, the students welcomed him or her by standing. In his treatise on pedagogy, al-Zarnūji devotes a whole section to the high regard in which a student should hold the profession of teaching. He wrote in 1203, "I am the slave of him who hath taught me even one letter."[5]

Children were taught profound respect for their parents and adults, and this pattern of respect for older people is still being practiced in the Arab and Muslim world. When the children grow up they become responsible for looking after the welfare of their parents and relatives. In the absence of the father, the brothers take care of the mother and unmarried sisters. I can attest to the fact that most Arabs are among the best family-oriented people in the world.

Arab Music

Apart from talking about God and teaching a variety of themes on biblical doctrines, music ranks very high on the list of topics which I love to discuss. Nevertheless, since this chapter is mainly concerned with a synoptic presentation of a few thought patterns and cultural practices of the Arabs, I must synthesize my thoughts in summary form.

Arab music is a consolidation of Persian and Syrian elements with the native musical style, which flourished in Arabia under the Umayyad Caliphs (661–750). Many treatises on music theory and history were written by such men as the philosopher al-Kindi and the illustrious al-Fārābi. Ibn-Misjah devised a system of modal theory that lasted throughout the Golden Age of Islam under the first Abbassid Caliphs (A.D. 755–850). Under the last Abbassid Caliphs, during the eleventh century, a strong Turkistan influence was brought into Arabian music by the Seljuks.

The chief characteristics of Arab music are modal homophony, florid ornamentation, and modal rhythm. The melodic modal system of ibn-Misjah contained, in its final form, eight modes. This system lasted until around the eleventh century, when the modes were increased to twelve, which were called *maqamāt*. Until that time the Arabian gamut consisted of twelve tones, roughly equal to the chromatic scale of Western music. But in the thirteenth century, five more tones were added, each a quarter tone below each diatonic whole tone. In the sixteenth century, a new tuning of the gamut was adopted, and the octave was divided into twenty-four quarter tones.

Ornamentation in Arab music consisted of shakes and trills, grace notes, appoggiaturas, and the tarkib, which was the simultaneous striking of certain notes together with the fourth, fifth, or octave—producing beautiful harmonic effect. Short melodies were repeated several times for each stanza, and each repetition was elaborately ornamented. Spanish music has been greatly influenced by Arab musical techniques. The main difference between the two styles of music is that the Spanish octave is equal to the chromatic scale of Western music, whereas the Arab octave consists of twenty-four quarter tones. There are many other distinguishing features of the two kinds of music.

The principal Arab instruments, other than those borrowed from Semitic cultures, were the long-necked tanbur and the short-necked lute called *oud*. The European lute derived its form and name from the *oud*. In fact, the *oud* is the ancestor of the Spanish guitar and other stringed instruments. History tells us that the Crusaders brought the *oud* from the Middle East to Europe. The *oud* has five to six double strings with no frets. We are also told that Arab music has exerted great influence on Spanish music, dancing, and singing.

Hearing Middle Eastern music for the first time, the uninformed Westerner might misjudge it as harsh, discordant, and monotonous. And when Muhammad Abd-el-Wahhab sings, although he is considered the greatest composer-singer the Arab world has ever known, his songs may seem to the uneducated Westerner as tremulous, endlessly mournful, and boring.

Understandably, Arab musical idioms and styles are as different as languages and customs, and if they cannot be understood they cannot be appreciated. The differences in Arab music do not occur because Arab composers are unaware of music theory and harmony, or because the musicians cannot read music. They occur because the octave is divided into twenty-four quarter tones rather than thirteen half tones, counting the root going upward chromatically to the octave, thus lending a peculiarly atonal quality that is so distressing and disappointing to Western ears.

There are equally good reasons for these differences that go back to an era when Arab music, not Western, reigned supreme in the world. I am happy to say that my musical training in Lebanon, Egypt, and the United States helped me develop an appreciation for good Eastern and Western music. I was trained by my Arab professors to trace my native folk forms all the way back to the Bedouins of ancient times, whose homely caravan song (the *huda*) consoled their lonely desert treks. Its meter corresponded to the rhythmic lurching stride of the camel and consisted of six metrical feet. Each foot was comprised of two longs, a short, and an accentuated long. This became the prototype of most Arab musical meters.

The Bedouins emphasized solo singing rather than instrumental music, due to the nomadic Arab life and tribal mobility which made it very difficult to carry musical instruments. On the other hand, instrumental music flourished throughout the Mediterranean littoral during the Golden Age of Islam. The Bedouins' style of singing and the introduction of melodic systems were added to simple and complex rhythmic modes.

The Arabs love to hear popular singers in the open gardens under the stars on balmy summer nights, where the audience is expected to give vent to its feelings by bursting forth with shouts of exhilaration and with applause of appreciation to good singing and orchestration.

Unfortunately, the raucous and rattling musical styles of modern times, coupled with the proliferation of wild rhythmic beats, have been transported by the ocean waves from the Atlantic and Pacific, spilling over on the shores of the Mediterranean Sea. These clumsy sounds have long reached and saturated Middle Eastern cities and were instrumental in polluting their traditional life-style, thus leading to unhealthy and ungodly habits. These destructive consequences are a far cry from the judicious artistic and moral influences that the West once gave to the world!

The Arab Woman

The West's knowledge of Arab women presumably started in Hollywood with Rudolf Valentino. However, from earliest recorded history, women have lived out their lives in the shadow of men. They were confined mainly to the home, treated as the property of their husbands, and used for pleasure and procreation.

Patriarchal society began with Adam and Eve. The patriarchal tradition has persisted in many societies, including that of the Middle East, though Arab women occasionally ruled as independent monarchs—the beautiful and alluring Queen of Sheba, the Egyptian queens acting as regents, and the famous Zenobia of Syria, for example.

In Greece, the "freewoman" took no part in public life and was constantly under the guardianship of her father or husband. The nomadic Hebrews were strongly patriarchal, and some of them had more than one wife.

During the Golden Age of Islam, veiling and seclusion of women were not generally practiced. During the eighth and ninth centuries A.D., the Abbassid era, Arab women wrote poetry and composed music and competed with men in cultural gatherings. Harun al-Rashid's wife, Zubaydah, appeared at many receptions attired in attractive jewels and brocades. In Muslim Spain, beautiful Arab ladies were seen dancing the *zambra* with their suitors. Some married women ruled the Arab empire behind the caliphs.

During the Middle Ages, non-Arab women in the Western world were not faring as well as the Arab women. In France and England, non-Arab women toiled long hours in unhealthy factories. Husbands could legally beat their wives and subjugate them, and would automatically take custody of the children in a divorce. As late as the Victorian Age, English women were not allowed to attend a university or vote.

Among many Western misconceptions is that concerning the Arab women, instantly placing them in a setting that is remote, poor, and faintly biblical. More often than not they are stolidly threshing wheat with an ancient flail, carrying a jug to the riverbank, and washing their family's dirty clothes with their bare hands.

These impressions are not entirely inaccurate, because along the banks of the Nile, the Tigris, and at other locations in the Middle East, thousands of women are still plodding silently through the ancient patterns which history has imposed upon them. However, elsewhere in the Near East such impressions bear little relation to reality.

It is not at all surprising nowadays to see suntanned women driving a golf ball down a fairway in Cairo, or a young woman on a horse galloping along the coast of Beirut, or even to see such conservative cities as Baghdad and Damascus offer facilities for both men and women to play tennis, and so forth.

Arab women are trained to serve their husbands and teach their children in the way they should go. Children are trained to honor their parents and to respect their elders. The father is the head and final authority of his household, and this authority is handed down to the oldest son. Arab women are stereotyped in the West as doormats for their husbands, but they are held in high esteem in the Arab home and have a great influence at home and in society. Since the family is greatly valued in the Arab world, the women cherish their roles as homebuilders and help shape the character of their children.

When Christian missionaries are able to lead an Arab

woman to a personal knowledge of our Lord and Savior, Jesus Christ, the same woman may become another "Lydia" (Acts 16:14). However, the Arabs frown on men talking to their women, especially if they are trying to proselytize them. Most Arab women are cared for and pampered by their husbands. Mutual respect is very important in the Arab home. Arab women find fulfillment in their role as wife and mother, and they do not compete with their husbands, but instead complement them.

However, some of these traditions are crumbling under the pull of modern technology and the pressure of Western materialistic standards. It appears that such pressures of modernization are affecting even the traditional Arab families. Comparatively speaking, and despite the negative things aforementioned, the modern Arab women and the traditional ones are among the most faithful and ingenious homebuilders in the world.

The Arab Mind

According to Islam the greatest contribution of the Arabs to man was in the spiritual realm which was offered on the verbal level. Muhammad was somewhat illiterate, yet he dictated the whole text of the Qur'an in perfect Arabic, whereby its rhetorical language has remained to this date the paragon in Arabic. The Arabs pride themselves on possessing a rich storehouse of oral literature consisting of legends, poetry, history, folk stories, riddles and songs, genealogies, sayings, and proverbs.

The Arab has a remarkable alertness of mind and does not usually carry his philosophy in books; he carries it with him. Rarely overtaken by unexpected events, his vivid imagination and brilliant memory help him unravel puzzling situations. The Arab loves to quote poems, anecdotes, parables, historical stories, and to switch from one topic to another, and weaves them into a semi-artistic whole. He is a romantic dreamer, gregarious and ceremonial.

Unhappily, the Arab is perceived primarily as a person of words rather than deeds. Much is promised and planned but little is carried out. There is far more talk than positive action. The enthusiasm for an enterprise that he launches is disproportionate to his readiness and willingness to effectuate it. The Arab has a fatalistic outlook on life, and his time is not regulated by the clock or by the calendar. He is fully aware that the Westerner has surpassed him technologically and has established legitimate superiority at a great emotional, physical, mental, and spiritual expense.

Islam's outlook on the present modern world and its future affects the attitude of the Arab toward a change that may lead to moral and spiritual decay, and he tries relentlessly to hold fast to the old ways of his forebears. He argues convincingly that the Christians in the West are deteriorating morally and spiritually with every passing generation, and becoming mechanized and automated. Thus Muhammad's teachings should be propagated in order to restore this sick world to health.

The Arab differs in so many ways from the Westerner. The reconciliation with his ambivalence toward a number of things could serve as an illustration. When the Arab appears to hate what he really loves, to refuse what he actually wants, to promise what he does not intend to carry out, and to vilify what he seeks to praise and commend—this would present him to the Westerner as incomprehensible and totally confused, while this behavioral pattern is a normal procedure of social life in the Arab world.

What to many Westerners may seem to be an instance of psychological disturbance, the Arab society would consider as a regular and healthy emotional trait. For instance, in trying to communicate a certain idea, the Arab may shout, get excited, and rebuke intensely. This would be interpreted by foreigners as being a belligerent situation, and the atmosphere would be charged with anger and hostility. On the other hand, this is the normal way some Arabs communicate with each other.

The way the Arab discusses the history of his family, his country, his religion, or mentions anything of which he is a part, he talks about them with excessive praise and boasts of them with exaggeration and assertion. In their prideful and exaggerated form, these traits may seem to a Westerner as a typical syndrome of a mildly megalomaniac paranoid. But in the Arab entourage they are simply characteristics of an accepted way of life.

The Arab is warm and enjoys interacting with people on a personal basis. He is outgoing and shows no signs of shame about his beliefs and ideas. He has been conditioned by his ethnic heritage to adjust to the most harsh treatment of life and people. He believes that these grueling circumstances were brought upon him by "fate." He does relegate to "Allah" his total destiny while he waits in resignation for the final day. This kind of total surrender to the will of God may suggest to a foreigner that this type of abnormal behavior is an obsessional neurosis.

The Arab is endlessly striving to live up to what he claims in public, and he is extremely attached to his ideal self. He is highly concerned about his reputation and family honor. His private life at home differs considerably from his formal social appearances. This would help create the discrepancy that is found between his private and public behavior. If the Westerner happens to observe these two contradictory traits by entering into the informal and formal gatherings of the Arab, he may declare that the Arab has a split personality.

At one occasion the Arab is responsive to the environmental stimuli, strongly emotional in his utterances and laughter, interacting intensely with the people and fanatically enthusiastic about the issues being discussed. At another occasion he is withdrawn into utter seclusion and complete silence, melancholic and apathetic with an amazing insensitivity to earthly sufferings, and surrendering with shocking indifference to the heaviest catastrophes in life. Observing these accentuated differences in an Arab may very well make a Westerner wonder at their similarity to some schizophrenic symptoms.

When I went back to Lebanon in 1968–70 as music educator, I befriended an American psychiatrist, who came to Beirut prospecting a successful practice. After about one year of dealing with his Arab patients and trying to figure out their incomprehensible temperament and thought patterns, based on Western psychiatric methods, he came to the sad conclusion that his efforts had been futile. Because of his distorted perception of the Arab mind, he eventually closed his practice and returned to America.

I have tried to formulate in this chapter a bird's-eye view of a few thought patterns and cultural practices of the Arabs, and in the process of doing so, I have prayed fervently that Almighty God would expose the misconceptions concerning the Arabs in particular, and that He would recondition Western political theology which has become a stumbling block to evangelism.

Furthermore, the political stance of so many European and American Christians toward Israel has had severe consequences. For instance, the Arabs have been perceived by most Christian fundamentalists and others as the enemies of God, and they have been viewed as mere pawns in a chess game of human history. More often than not they have been vilified and mortified by the mass media and by multitudes of publications, and their chronic conflict with Israel has convinced the zealots that the Arabs have been cursed by God.

Just because there is enmity between most Arabs and Jews, the Arabs are met by apathy and rejection in a number of Western circles, and their ethical qualities and cultural contributions have been perhaps intentionally ignored. And thus, more than one billion Arabs and Muslims have been cheated and deprived of hearing and believing a balanced biblical view of God's universal love.

These absorbing facts are promoting the spread of Islam here and abroad, and causing many nations to wonder at the disparity between the preaching of the gospel of Christ and the behavioral patterns of those who are doing the preaching. Observing similar kinds of disparity among the Christians of his day, Gandhi was reported saying, "If not for the Christians, I would have become a Christian!"

8

A Christian Response to Arabic Terrorism

Ask any average American about his or her opinion of Middle Eastern Muslims, and the answer would assuredly be that most of these Arabs are savages, or even crazy terrorists. Those who are not familiar with the Arabs and who depend on the press reports and on most televangelists can perhaps be excused for stereotyping the Arabs as being crazy terrorists and a cursed race. With this in mind, let us now try to consider some of the reasons for the brutal and insane acts of terrorism.

Terrorism is an ancient enigma which can be traced to the time of Abel and Cain, when "Cain rose against Abel his brother and killed him" (Gen. 4:8). Since that time, millions of innocent human beings have been killed or crippled by terrorist acts for much less or more reasons than jealousy.

In modern times terrorism is being used to underscore the vulnerability of the target government to accomplish an objective. Terrorism is a means to an end. It is the systematic use of violence in order to achieve social, political, or national goals. It is a phenomenon distinct from acts of war or crime. The goal of a common criminal is to kill at will for personal physical and emotional satisfaction. War is a declared state of armed conflict between two or more nations. But a terrorist's goal is to mold world opinion in favor of his cause, whether it be legal or illegal.

Shakespeare wrote in *Hamlet* that "all the world is a stage and the men are merely players." The terrorist undoubtedly uses this approach as a morality play so he can plead his cause to a worldwide audience. We see this kind of morality play being practiced in many countries, such as Ireland, Lebanon, and Israel. Not only that, but each year the number of terroristic attacks throughout the world grows drastically. Latin America leads the world in terroristic activities, and terrorism has become an international addiction.

Terrorism has emerged as the single threat to our world's stability. According to *U.S. News and World Report,* there are now at least ten incidences per day of terrorism, which are up from ten per week in 1970. These statistics include terrorist acts here in America. These activities are motivated by underground left-wing and right-wing extremists who often encourage illegal terroristic acts. Among these organizations are the Revolutionary Communist party, the Socialist Workers party, the Progressive Labor party, the Ku Klux Klan, the Nazi party, the Black Liberation party, the Christian Patriotic Defense League, and many others. All of them are Americans who are anti-democratic. Some of these radical organizations have committed various kinds of terroristic acts in this country.

Terrorism is derived from a Greek word meaning "to tremble." It was an old state-sponsored weapon used in the French Revolution, dating back to 1793–94. The English statesman Edmund Burke said that "thousands of those hell hounds called terrorists were turned loose by the state against the populace." Every country in the world has practiced and still is practicing terroristic acts in diverse places. Speaking on terrorism in Palestine, David Lamb wrote in his book, *The Arabs*, the following observation:

> When British rule was coming to an end in Palestine, both the Arabs and the Jews practiced terrorism against one another, and against the British. Jewish terrorists killed 338 British citizens in Palestine during the 1940s. They blew up the King David Hotel, the British headquarters in Jerusalem, in 1946, killing ninety-one persons, and perfected the lethal letter bomb. . . . I have in my files a photostat of a WANTED poster issued by the British colonial authorities about 1943. It shows the mug shots of ten men hunted as terrorists, pictured in alphabetical order; the first is that of a Polish clerk whose "peculiarities" are listed as "wears spectacles, flat footed, bad teeth." His name was Menachem Begin, and he and his colleague, Yitzhak Shamir, also a suspected terrorist, were to become future prime ministers of Israel. Begin would also become a winner of the Nobel Peace Prize, sharing the award in 1978 with President [Anwar] Sadat. . . . The important point here, I think, is that the Arabs don't have a patent on terrorism. . . . When the United States shells Muslim villages near Beirut or bombs Libyan terrorist targets, killing civilians in the process, Washington may view the act as one of retribution, but those on the receiving end surely consider it terrorism. Israeli air raids that kill innocents in Palestinian villages may be carried out in the name of self-defense, but to the recipients—indeed to the Arabs as a whole—that is just a euphemism for terrorism. Why, they ask, is violence condoned as justified when undertaken by one group and condemned as uncivilized barbarity when committed by another? Terrorism executed at thirty thousand feet may be impersonal, but surely it's just as deadly as an assassin's bullet fired from a speeding car.

Terrorism has become a way of life in Lebanon as never before. No one can really fathom what it is like to live in a country where life and death coexist. Every generation has witnessed its own war, but this present generation has had the biggest share of carnage and suffering. Parents have become reluctant to give birth to children who may end up victims of terroristic acts. Western media often reports the seemingly unending turmoil in Lebanon, but the true story of Lebanon's apparent disintegration remains untold.

America was still regarded as a friend before it was sucked into the labyrinth of violence. When the United Nations Security Council condemned Israel's invasion of Lebanon and its subsequent bombardments of Beirut during the summer of 1982, the United States of America not only vetoed the United Nations Security Council's resolutions, but President Reagan sent the American fleet and the marines to support Israel's interests in Lebanon and to protect the Lebanese "Christians."

A unit of the Lebanese "Christian" army was besieged by Muslim militiamen in a small mountain village above Beirut. The presence of the marines and naval ships off the seacoast of Lebanon, gave the "Christians" a feeling of relief and a sense of temporary security, or so it seemed.

Apparently President Reagan and his advisers had already forgotten how much America had been humiliated by the Vietnamese guerillas. The same mistake was repeated in Lebanon when the U.S. warships opened fire on Muslim positions, killing innocent citizens in the process. The world's largest battleship, the *New Jersey*, terrorized Muslim villages and others with its one-ton rounds. The exploding shells of the *New Jersey*, the rumble of canons, the militia's activities of the U.S. marines, and the brutal bombardments of Beirut by the Israeli army—all these have created a new anti-American terrorist!

Early one morning in October, 1983, a Shiite Muslim was seen circling in a parking lot near the U.S. marines' base in Beirut. He was driving an old yellow Mercedes-Benz truck that was loaded with more than six tons of high explosives. The guard on the marines' base had no good reason to worry or become suspicious, because he did not know what was in the truck, and also because the base was located near the international airport where many cars and trucks drove through that area frequently.

On that morning of October 23, the sun was just rising over the horizon of the Mediterranean Sea when the truck made a swift turn and crashed through the steel gate of the base and slammed with great force into the marines' battalion headquarters, killing 241 American marines. The guard reported that the truck driver looked right at him and smiled as the truck raced past the guard post.

The truck driver was a committed Shiite Muslim who died as a martyr for a "holy cause." The Qur'an promises those who give their lives for a holy and just cause will be greatly rewarded in heaven. The Qur'an says, "Who fighteth in the way of Allah be he slain or be he victorious, on him we shall bestow a vast reward."

Let us remember that such acts of discriminant terrorism have been encouraged by the selfish and brutal behavior of foreign powers, whose motives are to exploit weaker nations and to subjugate them by coercion for self-interests. Terrorists are not born, they are made—and no one can make them better than the Palestinian shantytowns (refugee camps) in Israel and in Lebanon's Sabra and Chatilla.

I have been asked over and over again by my students and others, "Why do the Arabs hate us Americans?" I answer them by simply saying that the Arabs do not hate the Americans as a whole, but the Arabs believe that the United States has lost its interest in playing a neutral peacemaker's role in the Middle East, and pledged to support Israel's inhumane political policies, at the expense of ignoring the Palestinians' human rights.

In his 1796 farewell address, President George Washington admonished the young republic to be neutral and to "observe good faith and justice toward all nations." America's founding fathers knew very well what they were talking about. Freedom is precious, especially the freedom to determine one's own destiny. The young republic defeated a much more powerful nation, mainly because they were fighting for a just and holy cause. I believe that the U.S. would do well to heed Washington's advice and restore the original American dream by playing a neutral peacemaker's role, especially in the Middle East. Otherwise, terrorism will flourish and will become an infringement on the rights of the innocents who would like to live in peace.

The long-range solution to terrorism would not be to strike back against it by the use of force, as many nations have done, because the use of force ordinarily backfires and leads to more terrorism. Only the guilty must be sought after and punished. When President Reagan ordered the bombing raid on terrorist facilities in Tripoli and Benghazi, with the intention to kill Moammar Kadafi, more than fifty innocent civilians died in the attack and many more were wounded. Every time Israel retaliated on terroristic attacks, more innocents were killed and the level of violence increased rather than decreased.

What is, then, the long-range solution to terrorism? Before trying to expound upon this important question, I would like to encourage the reader to prayerfully ruminate on the following criteria. Should the Christians in the Western world give an almost exclusive endorsement to the welfare of the state of Israel, without giving the Palestinians an equal right to determine their destiny in their own homeland? And what would the Christians' response be to terrorist activities between the Arabs and Jews?

Ironically, the belief that the creation of the physical Israel in 1947 was the fulfillment of biblical prophecies has been promulgated by a multitude of American televangelists and other Western Christians, and has encouraged Israel's determination to uproot the Palestinians from their homeland. Moreover, this has also contributed to the popular support for the U.S. government's pro-Israeli policies.

Undoubtedly the root of terrorism between the Arabs and Jews could be traced to the illegal seizure and occupation of Palestine by the European Jews, coupled with the mounting treacherous treatment of the Palestinians. More than that, around 40 million Christians have been conditioned by Western political theology to support Israel's exclusive claim to the land of Palestine, and countless pulpits are being used as a launchpad to promote the financial and political support of Israel. What is really burdening my mind and grieving my heart is not the support of Israel, but the prejudicial malice that is festering in the hearts of most American Christians toward the Arabs and Muslims, and especially the Palestinians.

Case in point, a former White House staff writer, Grace Halsell, who has published twelve books, deals with Christian Zionism in *On the Road to Armageddon: Crusaders for a Nuclear War* by saying:

In June, 1981, seated in my apartment in Washington, D.C., I listened to Israeli Prime Minister Menachem Begin being interviewed on American television. He had just ordered a strike on the Iraqi nuclear facility. The attack resulted in a few Americans questioning his use of the U.S.-supplied F-16 bombers for a raid on a sovereign Arab country. What about this criticism, he was asked. He was not worried, he replied. Israel had many friends. Israel, he added, had the support of 40 million Christians . . . to silence any criticism of the raid on Iraq, he placed an urgent phone call for help . . . to the Rev. Jerry Falwell. "Get to work for me," he told Falwell. Falwell said he would—and added: "Mr. Prime Minister, I want to congratulate you for a mission that made us very proud that we manufacture those

F-16s. In my opinion you must've put it right down the smokestack." ("North American Scene," *Christianity Today,* Aug. 7, 1981). In the year that I heard Begin boast of Israel having the support of 40 million Christians, I began to research Christian Zionism. And I became convinced that Begin was right: Christian support of Israel is more important than Jewish support to the Zionist state. There may be six million American Jews who support Israel, but there are about 40 million Christians who do. . . . let me say that I came to the study of Christian Zionism from a background of fundamentalism. . . . If the Bible says it, we are told, do not use your mind. Accept it as God's truth and God's will. . . . The Jews were God's Chosen People. And God gave the Holy Land to His Chosen People, the Jews. And because the Jews were His Chosen People, God would bless those who blessed the Jews and curse those who cursed the Jews. . . .

Early in 1985, I signed to go on another Falwell-sponsored tour. . . . Although we would be 850 Christians traveling to the Land of Christ, Falwell in his brochure made not a single mention of Christ. . . . We proceeded to Jerusalem, where Falwell chose to honor Ariel Sharon. All 850 of us gathered for the occasion. In introducing Sharon, Falwell said that in the annals of history, only a few great men came along. He named George Washington, Abraham Lincoln—and Ariel Sharon!

In 1983, Falwell had honored then defense minister Moshe Arens. Arens praised the Israeli invasion of Lebanon—which killed and wounded tens of thousands of Palestinians and Lebanese, most of them civilians, and said the United States should back Israel in future wars—"to wipe out the enemies." Falwell and the Christians jumped to their feet, applauding and shouting "Amen" and "Hallelujah!"

I realize that all of us who take the Bible seriously must love Israel, not only for being chosen prophetically, but also because God commanded us to "go therefore and make disciples of all the nations. . . . Go into all the world and preach the gospel to every creature. . . . and that repentance and remission of sins should be preached in His name to all nations, beginning at Jerusalem. . . . and in all Judea and Samaria, and to the end of the earth" (Matt. 28:19; Mark 16:15; Luke 24:47; Acts 1:8).

In spite of their frequent trips to Israel, Western evangelical Christians do precious little missionary work in the land where Jesus walked. The Israeli government encourages many evangelists to propagate a racial and political gospel in favor of Israel, as long as the gospel of Christ stays out of Jerusalem, Judea, and Samaria.

The apostle Paul was "not ashamed of the gospel of Christ, for it is the power of God to salvation for everyone who believes, for the Jew first and also for the Greek" (Rom. 1:16). Apparently, a number of Christians are a silent majority when it comes to preaching the gospel of truth in Israel, and they are obeying the Israeli government, rather than God, to not "speak at all nor teach in the name of Jesus" (Acts 4:18)!

As an ordained minister of the gospel of our Lord and Savior Jesus Christ, I genuinely love the Jews as much as I love the Arabs, but I hate both of their evil deeds and terroristic activities. However, since I love the unconverted Jews, if I fail to see them primarily as unrepentant people, I become guilty of inoculating them with false hopes of salvation and forgetting the desperate spiritual blindness engulfing Israel today.

Conversely, during my missionary journey to Israel in 1982, I attended a meeting where Western and European Christian speakers reviewed the horrors of the holocaust in Germany. They stressed the belief that since the Jews are so different from the Arabs, they must live exclusively among Jews. An Israeli Jew, seated in the audience, rose to his feet and suggested that many Israelis now would be willing to trade territory confiscated in 1967 for peace with the Palestinians. In answer to that, a noted Christian leader shouted with excitement: "We don't care what many Israelis say, we care what God says, and God gave the land to His chosen people the Jews, and all the Arabs must leave this land!"

Moreover, many Jews from time to time will criticize Israel's belligerent treatment of the Palestinians, and even call for an independent Palestinian state. But Christian Zionists are more loyal and fanatical supporters of militant Zionism than are many Jews, because they "think that" they are doing "God service" (John 16:2)!

I met a converted Jew at the Stella Kermil Hotel in Isfiyah, who called himself a Messianic Jew. He invited me to his home for lunch and fellowship, and took me to the evening service at the Messianic Temple in Haifa. Most of the worshippers were Messianic Jews, and the rest were Palestinians and others. These believers conducted their worship services on Saturday evening in the Hebrew language. It was so exciting to see the Messianic Jews and the Palestinians singing and praising their mutual Lord and Savior Jesus Christ, side by side, in perfect harmony and brotherly love.

This is what the true Church of Christ is all about. The New Testament teaches that there are only two kinds of churches: (1) the local church; and (2) the universal Church. The local church is seen in local assemblies that have been redeemed by the shed blood of our Lord and Savior Jesus Christ, and the universal Church is comprised of all the redeemed worldwide (John 17:20–26).

The etymological meaning of the word *church* in the Greek is *ekklesia*. *Ekklesia* is made up of two words from the verb *ekkaleo*: *Ek*, meaning out; and *kaleo*, to call or summon. The two words together mean to call out. However, in the New Testament secular Greek, *ekklesia* signified an assembly hall or meeting place, where people gathered together to discuss or debate social and political issues (Acts 19:32, 39,

41). The same word was used in the Septuagint to denote a gathering of people for almost any type of activity. Later on, the disciples of Christ interpreted the word as applying to believers assembled together to worship the Lord Jesus and also to fellowship. And then, *ekklesia* became known as the universal Church of Christ, whether believers assemble together or not (Acts 8:1–3).

The Church is also known as the Body of Christ. This was a hidden spiritual mystery, "which from the beginning of the ages has been hidden in God who created all things through Jesus Christ" (Eph. 3:9). The apostle Paul defines this sublime mystery in Ephesians 3:6: "that the Gentiles should be fellow heirs, of the same body, and partakers of His promise in Christ through the gospel." The mystery here concerns the Gentiles and consists of their equal spiritual position and privilege in Christ by means of the gospel. In other words, Paul is saying that only regenerate Jews and Gentiles are able to share equal spiritual blessing. To say it differently, the Body of Christ is comprised of Jews and Gentiles who are baptized by the Holy Spirit at the very moment of salvation. First Corinthians 12:13 asserts that the prime requisite for entrance into the Body of Christ is baptism of the Holy Spirit. Romans 8:9 supports this truth: "Now if anyone does not have the Spirit of Christ, he is not His." The Body of Christ is an organism, not an organization. This is what I witnessed in Haifa when I saw the converted Arabs worshipping their mutual Lord and Savior, Jesus Christ, with the Messianic Jews.

I was told that there were about twenty-five Christian congregations throughout Israel—made up of nearly 4,000 Jews and many more thousands of Arabs. Both groups of believers risk family persecution and government harassment. However, Jewish and Christian Arabs love one another in Christ, and their bold witness in the midst of strong opposition was very inspiring to me.

What was more inspiring was the fact that the Palestinians and the Israeli Jews ought to be bitter enemies, yet the love of Jesus Christ united them. Such love is a major part of the answer to the Christian response to terrorism, and to peace in the Middle East in particular. If Western Christian Zionists are interested to be a part of that answer, they must strive fervently to balance their love for the physical Israel with their obedience to the Great Commission. Prophetic politics cannot be a substitute for the proclamation of the gospel of Christ in Israel!

I can attest to the inescapable fact that the most viable answer to the solution to terrorism is found in the New Testament. Only God is able to recondition the depraved heart of a terrorist and to transform him into a loving and forgiving person. The New Testament teaches that God hates all evil activities, including man's inhumane actions toward other human beings—but He loves the terrorists and His love embraces the entire human race regardless of color or nationality, or whether people are good or bad.

On February 18–20, 1986, the directors of the Navigators and Campus Crusade for Christ ministries sponsored meetings at Clemson University at which I spoke on terrorism. My lectures were followed by a time for discussion and questions. After lecturing in the various classes and in Sirrine Auditorium, 2" x 4" cards were given to students for their comments on my lectures. Here are some of the remarks: A young lady said, "I have never been to a more informative and interesting lecture. The speaker gave me new insight on this matter of the Jews and Arabs." Another student said, "I have been faced with such questions from my Arab friends. And, as a Christian, am asked to defend my God who can promote such hatred. Now, I feel more confident and knowledgeable to approach such questions." One Jewish student wrote, "Good talk. In a world that is so replete with hatred, in a universe where individuals/groups/

nations vie for supremacy, what can you expect in terms of peace? We need God's help and I regret the situation in the Middle East." A Christian student commented, "Dr. Hamada's message is truth. I too have grown up hearing those old lines about Israel. Great lectures like this are very much needed for Christians. Dr. Hamada is a bold man; we need many like him. One of our major problems is our inability to look at international problems from other than an American perspective. Our answers rest in the Word of God." There were many more positive and encouraging comments, and only a very few negative but polite ones.

Similar reactions are being expressed by the majority of North Americans. People are beginning to see that the preoccupation with biblical prophecy and the idolization of the physical Israel, these are diverting the attention of most Christian preachers and their faithful flocks from God's wonderful plan of salvation. According to the New Testament, God has two main plans for mankind: (1) God loves the whole human race, and He is "not willing that any should perish but that all should come to repentance" (2 Peter 3:9). And (2) God will judge all unbelieving Jews and Gentiles "whose names have not been written in the Book of Life of the Lamb slain from the foundation of the world. . . . And the smoke of their torment ascends forever and ever; and they have no rest day or night" (Rev. 13:8; 14:11).

God's judgment will fall on everyone who refuses to submit his or her heart to Christ. The book of Revelation concludes with the assurance that all those who believe in Christ shall live forever with Him in heaven, where there will be no more death, pain, or sorrow (21:4)!

I am quite sure that most of the Christian Zionists have at least a basic knowledge of the Bible. I am equally sure that they believe that God will judge those who do not accept the free gift of salvation, through the shed blood of Jesus Christ on the cross of Calvary, whether they be Jews or Gentiles. If this is so, why then are they provoking the Arabs to wrath by taking a political side with Israel, and neglecting to proclaim the gospel of salvation to both Arabs and Jews, especially in Israel? With this in mind, how can the unregenerate Arabs, Jews, and Gentiles escape the wrath of God if they "neglect so great a salvation" (Heb. 2:3)?

The term *Zionism* refers to a political Jewish movement for the establishment of a national homeland in Palestine for the Jews that have been dispersed. On the other hand, a Christian Zionist is a person who is more interested in helping God fulfill His prophetic plan through the physical and political Israel, rather than helping Him fulfill His evangelistic plan through the Body of Christ, beginning "in Jerusalem, and in all Judea and Samaria, and to the end of the earth" (Acts 1:8). Samaria (modern Nablus) is an Israeli town which is populated with Palestinians who need to be evangelized. To leave them unevangelized is to cheat them from inheriting eternal life and receiving their citizenship in heaven (Phil. 3:20).

I am happy to say that I have met several Western Christians who have influenced my life and helped me overcome many obstacles. The number of such friends has grown immensely. These Christians are known by their love, and love is a verb of action, meaning that they are practicing genuine faith in Christ.

On the other hand, I know other Christians who have an intense dislike for the Muslims, and particularly for the Palestinians. I have asked some of them for the reason for disliking the Arabs. More often than not they say to me, "because the Arabs are Israel's enemies, therefore, they are the enemies of God." Then, I say to them, if this is how you really feel about the Arabs, wouldn't you like to know what God says about His "enemies"? Here is what He said, "Love your enemies, bless those who curse you, do good to those who hate you, and pray for those who spitefully use you and persecute you" (Matt. 5:44). After reviewing the truth of the matter and discussing the Arabs and Muslims from God's point of view, my Christian friends leave with a reconditioned heart toward the Arabs and Muslims.

In conclusion, terrorism must be dealt with from a biblical approach. The Bible says, "Bless those who persecute you. . . . Repay no one evil for evil" (Rom. 12:14, 17). I have heard about Christians who have won many of their captors to Christ by their compassion and prayers for them. I can also speak on that from my own experience. God gave me love for those who had killed my parents, and after spending some time with one suspected killer, God gave me compassion for him and not hate.

"Bless" is *eulogia* in Greek. Eulogize is derived from *eulogia*, meaning to speak well of a person and not to curse (Rom. 12:14). We should leave all judgments of terroristic acts to God, mainly because He said, "Vengeance is Mine, I will repay" (Rom. 12:19). Furthermore, the government is responsible to protect the citizens from criminal acts. The Bible declares, "There is no authority except from God, and the authorities that exist are appointed by God" (Rom. 13:1). The government's function is to protect the citizens against evil activities, to punish the evildoers, and to promote the general welfare of the country. Christians are exhorted to pray for the political leaders, and "for all men . . . who are in authority, that we may lead a quiet and peaceable life in all godliness and reverence. For this is good and acceptable in the sight of God our Savior" (1 Tim. 2:1–3)!

The Christians who are mainly concerned with evangelism, rather than with political theology, can honestly declare with the apostle Paul at the end of their lives: "I have fought the good fight, I have finished the race, I have kept the faith. Finally, there is laid up for me the crown of righteousness, which the Lord, the righteous Judge, will give to me on that Day, and not to me only but also to all who have loved His appearing" (2 Tim. 4:7–8). Therefore, our wonderful Lord and Savior Jesus Christ determines that His children persevere to the end in faith, hope, and love, but the greatest of these is *Love!*

In conclusion, I look forward with great anticipation to being in fellowship with Abraham, Hagar and Ishmael, Sarah and Isaac, and with "a great multitude which no one could number, of all nations, tribes, peoples, and tongues, standing before the throne and before the Lamb [Jesus Christ], clothed with white robes, with palm branches in their hands, and crying out with a loud voice, saying, 'Salvation belongs to our God who sits on the throne, and to the Lamb!'" (Rev. 7:9–10).

Notes

Chapter 2 The Semitic Arabs

1. Robert Young, *Young's Analytical Concordance to the Bible* (New York: Funk & Wagnalls, 1936), 287.
2. *Ibid*.
3. Philip K. Hitti, *History of the Arabs*, tenth edition (New York: St. Martin's Press, 1970), 8.
4. *The New King James Version, Biblical Cyclopedic Index* (Nashville: Thomas Nelson Publishers, 1985), 155.
5. William Whiston, *Josephus* (Grand Rapids: Kregel Publications, reprinted, 1980), 32.
6. William Smith, *Dictionary of the Bible*, vol. 1 (Cambridge: Riverside Press, H. O. Houghton & Co., 1868–70), 136–42.
7. *Ibid*.
8. Ibn-Qutaybah, *Uyûn al-Akhbār* (Cairo: vol. iii, 1930), 209–13.
9. Hitti, *op. cit.*, 42.
10. Louis Bahjat Hamada, *God Loves the Arabs, Too* (Nashville: Winston-Derek, 1988), 26.
11. Smith, *op. cit.*
12. Hitti, *op. cit.*, 42.
13. Hitti, *op. cit.*, 149.
14. Hitti, *op. cit.*, 43.
15. Hamada, *op. cit.*, 83.
16. Hitti, *op. cit.*, 52.

Chapter 3 God's Encounter with Hagar

1. C. L. Woolley, *Ur of the Chaldees* (Penguin Books, 1940). Cf. Woolley, *The Sumerians* (1928, reprinted 1971).

2. Leon Wood, *A Survey of Israel's History* (Grand Rapids: Zondervan, 1970), 42.
3. *Ibid.*, 29.
4. Louis Bahjat Hamada, *God Loves the Arabs, Too* (Nashville: Winston-Derek, 1988), 93.
5. *Ibid.*, 103.
6. *The Jewish Encyclopedia*, vol. vi (New York: Funk & Wagnalls, 1902), 138.
7. *The Soncino Chumash* (New York: The Soncino Press, 1947), 75–134.
8. Pirke de Rabbi Eliezer, *The Ten Trials of Abraham*, translated by G. Friedlander (New York: Bloch, 1916), 190–191.
9. At Genesis 16:1, cited in Friedlander, *ibid.*, 190.
10. Hamada, *op. cit.*, 91.
11. *The New King James Version, Archaeological Discoveries* (Nashville: Thomas Nelson Publishers, 1985), 1380.
12. Nelson Glueck, *Rivers in the Desert* (New York: Farrar, Straus and Cudaly, 1959), 63.
13. *The Wycliffe Bible Commentary* (Chicago: Moody Press, tenth printing, 1974), 22.

Chapter 4 Ishmael, Prince of the Desert

1. William Whiston, *Works of Josephus*, vol. ii (Grand Rapids: Baker Book House, fourteenth printing, 1988), 96.
2. Richard Longenecker, *Biblical Exegesis in the Apostolic Period* (Grand Rapids: Eerdmans, 1975), 127.
3. *Ibid*.
4. Donald Grey Barnhouse, *Genesis: A Devotional Commentary*, 2 vols. (Grand Rapids: Zondervan, 1970), 1:126.
5. H. C. Leupold, *Exposition of Genesis*, 2 vols. (Columbus, Ohio: Wartburg, 1942; reprint, Grand Rapids: Baker, 1979), 1:500–501.

Chapter 5 The Making of a Great Nation

1. William Whiston, *Josephus* (Grand Rapids: Kregel Publications, reprinted, 1980), see foreword.

2. Ibraham Rif'at, *Mir'āt al-Haramayn*, vol. I (Cairo, 1925), 56–60.

3. Henry H. Halley, *Halley's Bible Handbook*, twenty-fourth edition (Grand Rapids: Zondervan Publishing House, 1965), 765.

4. Philip K. Hitti, *History of the Arabs*, tenth edition (New York: St. Martin's Press, 1974), 120.

5. Robert Roberts, *The Social Laws of the Qorin* (London, 1925).

6. C. C. Torrey, *The Jewish Foundation of Islam* (New York, 1933), 90, 102.

7. Louis Bahjat Hamada, *God Loves the Arabs, Too* (Nashville: Winston-Derek, 1988), 52.

8. Hitti, *op. cit.*, 206.

9. Hitti, *op. cit.*, 572.

10. C. A. Nallino, *Celestial Sphere* (Cairo, 1911), 281.

11. Friedrich Dieterici, *Die Philosophy der Araber* im IX. und X. Jahrhimdert n. Chr., vol XiV (Leyden, 1890), 66–83.

12. *Ibid*.

13. Ed. Maurice Bouyges (Beirut, 1930); tr. S. Van Den Bergh, 2 vols. (Oxford, 1954).

14. Hitti, *op. cit.*, 584.

15. William Osler, *The Evolution of Modern Medicine* (New Haven, 1922), 98.

Chapter 6 The Arab World

1. C. S. Coon, *Caravan: The Story of the Middle East* (New York: Henry Holt & Co., 1951–, 343.

2. Louis Bahjat Hamada, *God Loves the Arabs, Too* (Nashville: Winston-Derek, 1986), 74.

3. Sania Hamady, *Temperament and Character of the Arabs* (New York: Twayne Publishers, 1960), 229.

4. Hamada, op. cit., 80.

5. Philip K. Hitti, *A Short History of the Near East* (New York: D. Van Nostrand Company, Inc., 1966), 47–49.

6. Hamada, *op. cit.*, 43.

7. Kathleen M. Langley, *The Industrialization of Iraq* (Cambridge: Harvard University Press, 1961).

8. Fahim I. Qubain, *The Reconstruction of Iraq, 1950–1957* (New York: Frederick A. Praeger, 1958).

9. Philip K. Hitti, *History of Syria, Including Lebanon and Palestine* (New York: McMillan Co., 1951).

10. Philip K. Hitti, *History of the Arabs*, tenth edition (New York: St. Martin's Press, 1974), 458.

Chapter 7   Understanding the Arab Mind and Culture

1. See *Aramco World Magazine*, March–April 1988.

2. Philip K. Hitti, *History of the Arabs*, tenth ed. (New York: St. Martin's Press, 1974), 43.

3. *Ibid.*

4. For a more comprehensive study of the Hajj, see the special issue of *Aramco World Magazine*, Nov.–Dec. 1974.

5. Khalil A. Totah, *The Contribution of the Arabs to Education* (New York: AMS Press, 1926), 67–76.

Subject Index

Abbassid
  Caliphs 149, 166
  period 159, 169
Abbassid Caliphate 151, 158
Abd Allah (chart) 113
Adb-Al-Rahmān 135
Abd Manaf (chart) 113
Abdel Mutaleb Shaybah (chart) 113
Abdullah 114
Abel 176
Abimael 47
  (chart) 43
Abimelech 47. See also tribes,
    non-Arab
Abraham 41, 50–51, 56, 107, 117,
    191
  adopted Eliezer 77
  agrees with Sarah 65, 103
  arrives in Haran 66
  birth of 63
  builds altar to the Lord 69
  in Canaan 56, 66
  casts out Hagar and Ishmael 92,
    99–104
  (chart) 43, 50–51, 55
  circumcized 92
  descendants of 68, 148
  in Egypt 71–77
  faith of 71, 77
  final destination of 65
  gifts to his sons 48, 55
  God's appearance to 65, 70, 93, 97
  God's plan for 67, 83
  heathen upbringing 63
  "the Hebrew" 40
  home of 150
  hospitality and generosity of 89,
    158
  Ishmael's return to 95
  leaves Haran 69
  leaves Ur 66
  marriages 55, 65, 76
  with the Pharaoh 69–75
  returns to Canaan 77
  sons of 50, 58, 65, 89, 97
  temperament of 102
  trials of faith 70, 73, 92, 104
Abrahamic Covenant 75
Abram 73. See also Abraham
Abu Dhabi 127, 147
Abu-Talib 112
Acropolis of Baalbek. See Baalbek
Adam 87, 155, 166
Adbeel 53
  (chart) 50
Adnan (chart) 113
Africa 48, 127, 132, 146. See also
    North Africa
Agur the Massite 53
Ahab, King 132
"Aida" 142
Ain-el-Qudeirat 78
Ajman 147
al-Akhtal 154
Akkadian language 63
al-Azhar 143
Alexander the Great 135
Algazel 122. See also al-Ghazzal
Algeria 127
Alhamissa (chart) 113
Alhazen 123. See also ibn-al-
    Haytham
Ali 115
  wife of 117
al-Jawf. See Doomat-el-Jendel
Allah 112, 125, 144, 173, 179
  Arab submission to will of 109,
    116
  unity and sovereignty of 109
  See also God

Almighty 63, 87, 97, 107
  appears to Hagar 80
  See also God
Almodad 43
  (chart) 43
  See also Mudad
alms, giving by Muslims 162
Alpharabius 122. *See also* al-Farabi
al-Qahira. *See* Cairo
al-Sham. *See* Damascus; Syria
Amarna Tablets 70
American Christians:
  malice toward Arabs and Muslims
    181
  opinion of Muslims 176
American missionary 27. *See also*
  Christian missionary
Aminah 112
Amytas 149
Angel of God. *See* Angel of the Lord
Angel of the Lord 80
  confronted Hagar 60, 79, 84, 106
  and Ishmael 97
  See also God
Antioch 119, 135, 152
Antipas, Herod. *See* Herod Antipas
Antipater 50
Antiquities of the Jews 102
Apostles, home of 116
Aquinas, Thomas 122
Arab beliefs and logic 161–164
Arab Caliphs 116
Arab cooking 159
Arab culture 159–174
  ignorance about 127
Arab gentlemen, virtues of 165
Arab mind 159–174
Arab music 166
  chief characteristics of 165
  differences in 167
  ornamentation in 167
  principal instruments 167
  Turkish influence on 165
Arab oil 128, 147
Arab proverbs 155
Arab Spain, perfume production in
  49
Arab women 169
  misconceptions about 170
  modern 170
  in Muslim Spain 170
  as rulers 169

Arab world 129–153
  importance of 119
Arabia (Arabah) 40–47, 56. *See also*
  North Arabia
Arabian desert 58, 67
Arabian Empire 149, 154
  age of 116
Arabian Gulf 63, 147
  petroleum wealth of 147
Arabian merchants 53
Arabian Nights 127
Arabian Peninsula 42, 53, 116, 135
Arabian poets 154
Arabian traditions 53
Arabian tribes:
  historical character of 45
  traced to 58
Arabic, literary, numbers, and
  scientific work introduced 152
Arabic Bible. *See* Bible
Arabic language 119, 154
  as *lingua franca* 117
Arabic poetry 130. *Ser also* poetry
Arabic terrorism:
  Christian response to 178, 191
  See also terrorism
Arabs:
  as barbarians 89
  called Moors 127
  characteristics of 45, 127, 173
  contributions to the world xv 109,
    119, 124, 154, 175
  converted to Christianity 39, 113
  creators of perfume 149
  education of children 165
  generosity and hospitality of 45,
    53, 112, 159
  God's blessings on 149
  God's love for 175
  golden age of 152
  great wealth of 109, 124, 149
  intermarriage of 132
  Islam affects on 162
  jealousy among 135
  meaning of the word 41
  misconceptions about 99, 175
  negative stories about x, 76, 87,
    110
  nomadic lifestyle of 41
  provoked by the Jews 189
  ruled Spain 128
  social etiquette 160

Arabs (cont.)
  terrorism 177–182
  unevangelized 63
Arabs, The 177
Arabs, Semitic. See Semitic Arabs
Aram 68, 152
  children of 68
Aramaean people 68, 152
Aramaic language 68
Aramco World Magazine 142, 147
Arens, Moshe 184
Aretas IV 51
Aristotle 123, 130
Arphaxad (chart) 43
Asenath 160
Asia 129, 136, 147
Asia Minor. See Turkey
aslama 117. See also Islam
Assyria 67
  used by God 113
Assyrians 132, 152
  supremacy of Syria 152
astronomy 123
  Ptolemaic tradition of 119
Athanasius 116
Athenians 53
Atlantic Ocean 119, 127
Augustine 116
Avenpace (Avempace) 124. See also
  ibn-Bajjah
Averroës 124. See also ibn-Rushd
Avicenna 123. See also ibn-Sina
Ayyoub. See Job

Baakline 19
Baalbek 54, 135, 152
  Acropolis of 55
Babylon 50, 149. See also Hanging
  Gardens of Babylon
Babylonia 67
  ancient 53
  era 149
Babylonians 132, 152
Baghdad 76, 121, 153–157
  women in 171
Bahira 113
Bahrain 128, 147
ibn-Bajjah (abu-Bakr Muhammad
  ibn-Yahja ibn-Bajjah) 125. See
  also Avenpace
Balkis. See Queen of Sheba

balsam 53
Baltic 133
Barnhouse, Donald Grey 105
Bathsheba 70, 100
al-Battani 120
Battle of Tours 136
bavith 53. See also beit sha'ar
Bedouins 41
  style of singing 168
  See also nomads
Be'er-la-hai-ro'i 78
Beer-Sheba (Beersheba) 78, 117, 125
Begin, Prime Minister Menachem
  180–183
Beirut 132, 138
  Israel's bombing of 179
Beit al-Hikmah. See House of Wisdom
beit sha'ar 53
Benghazi 181
beni. See Omran, Beni
Beni-Misma 53. See also Masamani,
  tribe of
Beni-Tameen 58
Berbers 128
Bereans xv
Bered 78
Bethel 69
beyn-en-nahrein 51
Bible 47, 58, 87, 94, 99, 107, 160,
  184, 190
  Arabic 39
  compares Lebanon 136
  erroneously taught 32
  inerrancy of 100
biblical approach to terrorism
  186–191
biblical prophecy:
  preoccupation with 189
  See also prophecy
biblical scholars 48, 59–63, 78, 87
  misleading the public 94
biblical texts. See Midrash
Bilhah 76
Black Liberation party 177
Black Stone 165
bless. See eulogia
Body of Christ 188
Bonaparte, Napoleon 147
Book of Life of the Lamb 78, 189
Bozrah. See Buseirah
British 152

Burke, Edmund 177
Buseirah 51
Byblos 130, 135

Cadiz 133
Cain 176
Cairo 140–145
  Hollywood of the Middle East 143
  women in 171
Caleb, the Edomite 160
Caliph 122, 158
Calvary 189
camels 128
Canaan 133
  son of 152
Canaan (city) 55, 66, 77, 92
Canaanites 40, 58, 70, 133. See also
  Phoenicians
Carchemish 152
Carthage. See Tunisia
Chalchis 53
Chaldaea (Chaldea) 51, 133
Chaldaeans 51
  intermarriage 58
Chaldee dictionary 40
Chaldees 64
chariots 140
charismatic swindlers 65
China 120, 127, 152
chirography 113
chosen people. See God, chosen
  people of
Christ:
  deity of 162
  love of 107
  virgin birth of 162
  See also Jesus
Christ child, gifts to 48, 148
Christian Copt 116
Christian missionary 160
  as undercover spies 27
  See also missionary
Christian Patriotic Defense League
  177
Christian Zionists. See Zionism
Christianity 117, 138, 163
Christianity Today 184
Christians:
  in Cairo 147
  dislike of Arabs 128, 179, 181
  division among 61, 117, 175

response to terrorism 181
  support of Israel 184
  See also American Christians;
    Western Christians
Church 187
  became Paganized 113
  lethargic 116
circumcision 92
Columbus, Christopher 128
concubinage 63
Cordova 125
Cradle of Civilization. See Iraq
Cross 69
Crusaders 150, 168
cuneiform, system of writing 53, 63,
  158
Cushite groups, intermarriage 50,
  58
customs:
  at time of Abraham 77
Cyprian 119
Cyprus, island of 133

Damascus 48, 53, 67, 153
  women in 170
Daniel 68, 109
Dark Ages 117
David, King 70, 99, 104, 117, 133,
  147
Dedan 59
Dedanites 58
de Lemartine, Alphonse-Marie-Louis
  de Prat 138
de Lesseps, Ferdinand-Marie 147
Descartes, René 122
Destruction of the Philosophers 122
Dhofar 148
Diklah 46
  (chart) 43
Dilmun. See Bahrain
disciples 152, 187
divine:
  command 100
  intervention 78
  sovereignty 61
Doomat-el-Jendel (Dumat al-Jandal)
  53. See also Dumah
Druze religion 20, 94, 138
Dubai 128, 147
Dumah 53
  (chart) 50

Eber (Abir) 41, 48, 55
   (chart) 43
Edom 49–52. See also Petra
Edomite Hadad 53. See also Hadar
   (Hadad)
Egypt 53, 58, 69, 77, 105, 117, 127,
   135, 141–146
   architectural wonders of 141
   founder of 43
   historical contributions of 140
   Hollywood of the Middle East 20
   See also Ham; Misr
Egyptian queens 168
Egyptians 70, 79, 140
   ancient records of 78
   called to prayer 145
   characteristics of 142
   knowledge of the Qur'an 142
   optimism of 142
ekklesia (ekkalea) 187. See also
   Church
El-Ahkaf 46
Elias (chart) 113
Eliezer, adopted son of Abraham 77
Eliezer, Pirke de Rabbi 73
El-Mes'oudee 50
El-Mudad. See Mudad
El Roi 90
England 132
Ephraim 107
Esau 49–52
eternal salvation 94, 110, 115, 130,
   135, 189
Eternal Son of God 61
Eth-Baal, King (Ithobalus) 133
Ethiopia 48, 55
Euclid 130
eulogia 191
Euphrates 47, 51, 63, 67, 151, 158
Europe 120, 128, 133, 147
evangelism:
   biblical approach for 39
   Christian concern with 191
   stumbling block to 175
evangelists 38, 184. See also
   televangelists
Eve 87, 167
everlasting life 61
evil 67
Exposition of Genesis 107
Ezekiel 53
Ezra 68

Faher (chart) 113
faith:
   God's testing of 65, 92
   Muslin profession of 163
Falwell, Jerry 182
al-Farabi (Muhammad ibn-Muhammad
   ibn-Tarkhan abu-Nasr al-Farabi)
   121, 154, 165. See also
   Alpharabius
al-Farazdaq 154
Farouk, King 22
   deportation of 23, 147
fasting by Muslims 162
father of a king 48
Fatimah 117
Fatimid rulers 144
Fatimid Caliphate 138
Fertile Crescent 116
flamenco music 131
Flood 70
Fowles, John 155
frankincense 43–48, 148
Freemasonry 35
French 152
   architecture 147
Fujairah 147

Gabriel, angel 114, 165
   appears to Muhammad 114
Gades 132. See also Gibraltar
Galatian 127
Gandhi, Mahatma 175
Garden of Eden 48, 149
Genesis, Book of 41
Gentiles 38, 67, 130, 188
   baptized by the Holy Spirit 186
   intermarriage with Jews 40
   pagans 40
Gerar 48
Gesenius, Wilhelm 53
Geshur 152
Ghaleb (chart)
Gharat al-Hira
al-Ghazzali 122, 144. See also Algazel
Gibbon, Edward 135
Gibralter 134
God, is Spirit 60
God:
   appears to Abraham 65, 70, 92
   appears to Hagar 62, 77–88, 102
   blessings on the Arabs 127, 149
   chosen people of 67, 131, 183

curse on Israeli tribes 45
errors about 99
faith in 87
grace and mercy of 70, 110
kingdom of 67
love of 63, 87
love for the Arabs xv, 92
plan for the world 76, 94, 189
power of 184
promises to Abraham, Hagar and
    Ishmael 68, 87, 94, 112, 124
sovereignty of 60, 71, 76, 80, 84
Word of 43, 55, 60, 70, 94, 109,
    189
Godhead 107
God's encounter with Hagar 62–82
gods, other 41, 63
God's will, submission to 87
gold 48, 148
golden age of Islam 88–111,
    118–122, 152, 166–169. See
    also Islam
Gomorrah 97
Goshen 73
gospel:
    of Christ 70, 184
    damage to 27
    preaching of 175
    of eternal salvation 70, 162, 189
    truth 70, 99
Graham, Billy 70
Greco-Macedonians 152
Greek 53, 133, 152
    civilization 124
    Empire 152
    philosophy 154
    works 130
Gulf of Eyleh 58

Ha-Agar 73. See also Hagar
Hadar (Hadad) 53
    (chart) 50
Hadoram 45
    (chart) 43
Hadramawt 124, 150
Hagar 43, 51, 56–60, 67, 78, 95,
    108, 140, 147, 191
    Angel of the Lord appears to 60,
    78, 106
    birth of son Ishmael 89
    cast from Abraham's household 89,
    101

(chart) 43, 51
given to Abraham 65
God appears to 78–89, 103
God's promises to 87, 124
as inferior to Sarah 99
journey through the desert 78, 103
marriage to Abraham 76
returns to Sarah 74, 83
runs from Sarah 60, 81, 102
Sarah's jealousy of 84, 98
Hagarenes 55
Haifa 186
Hajj 161–165. See also pilgrimage
Halsell, Grace 181
Ham 43, 132
Hamah 152
Hamal (chart) 113
Hamath. See Hamah
Hamathites 152
Hamitic 56
Hamlet 176
Hammurabi 149
ibn-Hanbal, Ahmad 144
Hanging Gardens of Babylon 149
Hannibal 135
Haran 40, 66, 78, 138
    location of 18, 67
    See also Syria
Haran (brother of Abraham) 65
harem 127
    of Pharaoh 70
Hashem (chart) 113
haute cuisine, birthplace of 157
Havilah 48
    (chart) 43
Hawran. See Haran
ibn-al-Haytham 123. See also
    Alhazen
Hazarmaveth (Hadramawt) 45
    (chart) 43
heaven, wrath of 73
Heber 43
Hebrew:
    language 70
    prophets 117
Hebrew Scriptures 152. See also
    Scriptures
Hebrews 132
    descended from Peleg 40
    See also Jews
Hebron 92, 97, 104. See also Mamre
Hegel 152

Hejer 55
Heliopolis. *See* Baalbek
Hellenistic culture 135
Herod Antipas 50
Herod the Great 50
Hijaz 47
Hiram 132
historians 43, 48, 56, 126
Hitler, Adolph 112
Hitti, Philip 53, 58
Hittites 152
holocaust 112, 183
holy cause, martyr for a 165
Holy Spirit 22, 83, 99, 138
   baptized by 187
   power of 35, 107
House of Wisdom 121
Hurrians 78
hypocrisy in churches 32

idolatry 63, 113, 135
   center of 67
Idumaea 50. *See also* Petra
Idumaeans 50
images, worship of 113
imagination, as gift from God 63
India 48, 127, 151
Indus River 118
intermarriage 40, 50, 58, 65, 132,
   160
Iran, recent turmoil in 117
Iraq 52, 127, 151
   history of 152
   modern 63, 147
   oil deposits in 149
   See also Mesopotamia; Ur
Isaac 48, 78, 113, 97, 103–107, 117,
   191
   birth of 97
   circumcised 97
   God's love and plan for 93
   with Ishmael 97
   the Promised Seed 104
   wives of 67
Iscah 65
Ishbak 58
   (chart) 55
Ishmael 43, 55, 60, 112, 117, 165,
   191
   Angel of the Lord appears to 97
   banished from Abraham's
      household 89, 101

birth of 75, 89
(chart) 50, 113
claims his inheritance 102
deprived of inheritance 94, 124
descendants of 89, 119
a great nation 50, 83, 87, 94, 107,
   112, 125
a gift from God 83
God's description of 88
God's plan and love for 93
journey in the desert 94, 103–107
named by God 90
Prince of the Desert 84–107
the promised seed 91–94
returns to Abraham 96
upbringing of 89
Ishmaelites 50–58
(chart) 50
intermarriage 58
Islam 94
   effects on Arabs 162
   call to prayer 127, 162
   and Christianity 162
   compassion toward Jews 112
   creed of 127
   cultural contributions of 119
   golden age of 111, 118–122,
      166–170
   holiest cities of 162
   an independent religion 118
   Ismaili branch of (*See* Ismaili)
   meaning of word 87, 110, 117
   outlook on present world 173
   pillar of 163
   reasons for success and growth of
      117, 163
   rise of 111–116, 125
   Shi'ite sect 117
   spread of 175
   teachings 112, 163
   two major groups 117
   unifies Muslims 112
   winning converts to 118
   is world influence 158
Islamic countries welcome Jewish
   refugees 112
Islamic Empire 120
Islamic history 155
Islamic Spain 119, 128. *See also*
   Muslim Spain
Ismail, Khedive 142
Ismaili 138

Israeli terrorists 179
Israel 76, 152, 175
  bombing of Beirut 179
  children of 73
  claim to Palestine 181
  invasion of Lebanon 36, 179
  spiritual blindness of 184
  support of U.S. for 181
Israelis:
  recent turmoil with Palestinians xiii
  terrorism of 178
Israelites 70
Ituraea 54
Ituraeans 55

jabal Tariq. See Tariq's mountain
Jacob 41, 76, 102
  God's appearance to 102
  wives of 68
Jacob's well 83
Jakeh 53
Jehovah 81, 92, 160
  appeared to Hagar 90
  visit to a woman 61, 81
  See also God
Jerah 45
  (chart) 43
Jerusalem 67, 83, 104, 132, 147,
    162, 183, 189
Jesus:
  Qur'an teachings about 112
  spoke Aramaic 68
  and the Syrophoenician woman
    130
Jethro, flock of 58
Jetur 54
  (chart) 51
Jewish:
  terrorists 178
  tradition 99
Jewish refugees 112
Jewish scholars 112
Jewish Temple 132
Jewish zealotry 102
Jews 67, 142
  baptized by the Holy Spirit 186
  in Cairo 147
  as chosen people 130
  criticize Israel treatment of
    Palestine 184
  cursing of 38
  illegal seizure of Palestine 181

intermarriage with Gentiles 41
  practice terrorism 178
  spoke Aramaic 68
  unconverted 70, 130
  western world's belief about 99
  See also Hebrews; Semitic Jews
Jezebel 132
Jihad 165
Joab 53
Job 48, 53, 162. See also Jobab
Jobab 49
  (chart) 43
John, the apostle 61, 110
John the Baptist 55
Jokshan 58
  (chart) 55
Joktan 41, 59
  (chart) 43
  descendants of 42, 119
  sons of 43–50
Joktanites 43–50
  (chart) 43
  intermarriage 58
Jonah, tomb of 150
Jordan 128, 152
Josephus, Flavius 42, 48, 65, 102,
    110
Joseph 59
  sons of 107
  wife of 160
Joshua 46
Judah 41, 161
  children of 53
  tribe of 162
  wife of 58
Judaism 110, 117
Judea 183, 189

Kaaba 43
Kaabah 165
Kadafi, Moammar 181
Kadesh 78
kaht 44
Kahtan 44. See also Joktan
Kaib (chart) 113
Karnak 141
Kedar 52
  (chart) 50, 113
kedem (kiddam) 55
Kedemah 55
  (chart) 51
Kelab (chart) 113

Kenaneh (chart) 113
Kepler, Johannes 122
Keturah 48, 58, 147
 (chart) 43, 55
 descendants of 120
 marriage to Abraham 55
 six sons of 55
Keturahites 56
 (chart) 55
Khadijah 115
ibn-Khaldun (Abd-al-Rahmān
 ibn-Khaldun) 44, 125
Khatchatourian, Aram 55
Khawlan 48
Khazimah (chart) 113
Khurdistan 76
al-Khwarizmi (Muhammad ibn Musa
 al-Khwarizmi) 121
Kinalua 152
al-Kindi (Abu-Yūsuf Ya'qūb ibn-Ishāq)
 122, 165
kings of Arabia 41
Kisheem 46
Kittim (Chittim). See Cyprus
Korchah, R. Joshua ben 73
Ku Klux Klan 176
Kuwait 128

Lamb, David 177
languages 63, 68, 155
Lanza, Mario 25
LaSor, Dr. William Sanford 110
Latin America 177
Law of Moses. See Moses, Law of
Lawrence, T. E. 142
Lawton, John 142
laylat al-qadr 114
Leah 76
Lebanese Christians 179
Lebanon 54, 128–138, 152
 in the Bible 136
 corruption in 27
 invaded by Israel 179
 strategic position of 130
 terrorism in 179
leben (laban) 138
Lemuel 53
Leupold, H. C. 107
Levant 131
Levantine strip 133
Lincoln, Abraham 184
"Linguistic Iron Curtain" 155

Longenecker, Richard 102
Lord 107
 plagued Pharaoh 73
Lot 66
Lu'ay (chart) 113
Luxor 141
Lybia 128
Lystra 120
Lydia 171

Machpelah 107
Madrakah (chart) 113
Mael (Mali) 48
Magi 147, 163
 gifts to Christ Child 148
Mahalath 51
Makan (Magan) 147
Makkah 114, 145, 164. See also
 Mecca
Malaga (Malaca) 133
Malek (chart) 113
Mamluks 147
Mamre 92, 97
Manasseh 107
maqamāt 165
Maqum (chart) 113
Marduk 150
Mariam (Mary) 112
Marib 45
Martel, Charles 136
martyrs 114
Mary, worship of 114
Mary, wife of Muhammad 117
Masamani 53
Massa 52
 (chart) 51
 See also Masani tribe
Massani tribe 53
Mecca 43, 54, 112, 117, 163
Medan 58
 (chart) 55
Medanites 58
medicine 125
Medina 112, 167
Mediterranean 128–135, 152
Medo-Persians 133, 152
memory 145, 165
Memphis 140
Mesha 43
Mesopotamia 40, 50, 55, 64–70,
 128–132
 food from 158

See also Iraq
Messiah 48, 135
Messianic Jews 185
Mibsam 53
   (chart) 51
Middle East 129, 150
   answer to peace in 187
   current crisis in x, 179–191
   customs 65, 84
   U.S. role in 179
Midian 58
   (chart) 55
Midianites 58
Midrash 73
Milcah 65
minarets 146
ministry 38
minqaf 149
Mir-at ez-Zaman 44
Mirbat 45
Mishma 53
   (chart) 50
ibn-Misjah 165
Misr (Mizri). *See* Egypt
missionary. *See* American missionary
Mizraim 42, 70
mocking. *See* tsachaq
Mohammedanism 113
Mongol Tartars 152
Monteux, Maestro Pierre 25
moon-gods 63, 68
Moors (Moor) 120, 130. *See also* Muslims
Morad, tribe of 42
Morocco 128
Mosaic Law 65, 76
Moses 58, 65, 70, 140
   inspired by God 99
   Law of 46
   wife of 160
Mount Ebal 46, 68. *See also* Obal
Mount Gerizim 68
Mount Lebanon 136, 152
Mud 63
Mudad (El-Mudad). *See* Almodad
Muder (chart) 113
Mued (chart) 113
muezzin 146
Muhammad Abd-el-Wahhab 167
Muhammad, prophet 53, 112, 145, 155, 165, 171
   ancestry 112

angel Gabriel appears to 114
birth of 112
birthday celebration 145
   (chart) 113
death of 117, 128
dictates Qur'an in Arabic 115, 120, 170
followers of 136
meaning of 112
successor of 117
as supreme ruler 117
unified Arabia 112
wives of 115
Murrah (chart) 113
music. *See* Arab music; Spanish music
music education in Lebanon 27
Muslims:
   American opinion of 177
   called Moors 120
   cultural contributions of 130
   disputes among 135
   domination of 120
   enjoy their faith 117, 145, 163
   giving alms 163
   God's love for 175
   holy book (*See* Qur'an)
   obey their prophets 117
   pilgrimage 164
   "prayer call" 146, 163
   scholars 162
   women in Spain 130
Muslim beliefs. *See* Arab beliefs
Muslim Spain 130, 155
   Arab ladies in 171
Muslim villages:
   terrorized by the U.S. 179
Mutalib, Abdul 111
al-Mutanabi 145, 155
myrrh 48, 148
mystery, spiritual 187

Nabat 51
   (chart) 113
Nabathaeans (Nabataean) 51. *See also* Nabat
Nabeet 51
Nablus 83, 189. *See also* Samaria
Nader (chart) 113
Nahor (brother of Abraham) 65
   (chart) 43
Nahor 68
Nahur (chart) 113

Najran 58
Nanna. *See* moon-gods
Naphish 55
   (chart) 50
Nasiriyah 63
Navigators and Campus Crusade for
   Christ 186
Nazareth 38
Nazi party 177
Near East. *See* Middle East
Nebajoth (Nebaioth) 51
   (chart) 50, 113
Nebi Yunus 150
Nebuchadnezzar 150
Negev 78
Nejd 45, 58
Neoplatonism 122
New Jersey, bombing of Beirut 179
New Testament 107, 112, 188
   answer to terrorism 186
New Yorker 31
Night of Power. *See laylat al-qadr*
Nile River 141, 147, 171
Nile Valley 128, 140
Ninevah 51, 68, 158
Nizar (chart) 113
Noah 32, 41
Nobel Peace Prize 179
nomadic lifestyle 41, 167
nomads 41
North Africa 118, 128, 136
North Arabia 162
Nuzi 76
Nuzi Tablets 77

oil 128, 148
   in Iraq 150
   See also Arab oil
Old Testament 49, 61, 97, 107, 117
   history 102
   Jewish commentary of *(See Soncino
      Chumash)*
   practice of prayer 163
   typology in 81
Oman 128, 147
Omran, Beni 55
*On the Road to Armageddon:
   Crusaders for a Nuclear War* 182
Ophir 48
   (chart) 43
Origen 117
Orontes River 152

Osler, Dr. William 125
Ottoman Empire, defeat of 135
Ottoman Turks 134, 152
Ottomans 152
oud 21, 122

Padan-Aram 68
paganism 114
Palestine 48–56, 68, 116, 128, 152
   Israel's claim to 181
   terrorism in 177
Palestinians:
   recent turmoil with Israelis 22,
      179–191
   rights ignored by U.S. 181
   unevangelized 189
palm trees 46
Palmyra 152
Paradise 165
Paran 78
Pascal 122
Patena 152
patriarchal traditions 169
Paul, the apostle 65, 87, 92, 97–102,
   152, 185, 191
Pauline hermeneutic 102
Peleg 41
   (chart) 43
pere 90
perfume 150
Persia 135, 163
Persian Gulf 58, 63
Persians 152. *See also* Medo-Persians
Peter the Hebrew 100
Petra 51
Pharaoh 53, 71
   daughter Hagar 74–78, 99
   gifts to Abraham 73
   gives Hagar to Sarah 74
   land of the 70
   plagues from the Lord upon 73
   princes of 70, 73
pharaohs 141
Philip the Tetrarch 55
philosophic thought 125, 155
philosophy 123
   of Arabs 171
   See also Greek philosophy
Phoenicians 134
   history of 132
   trading stations of 133
   See also Canaanites

Phoenicia 152. *See also* Lebanon
pilgrimage 164
plagues 73
Plato 122, 130, 141, 147
poetry:
  Arabian 115
  lyric 155
  written by Job 48
Poitiers 135
Politics 122
Pompey 55
prayers by Muslims 162
Prince of the Desert. *See* Ishmael
Prince of peace 135
progenitors, of Arabs and Jews 72
Progressive Labor party 177
Promised Land 66
Promised Seed 72, 89–94, 104
prophecy 94, 147
Providential protection 81
Ptolemy 120, 125, 130
purple dye 133
pyramid, monolithic bulk 63
Pyramid Texts 70
Pyramids 70
Pyramids of Giza 141, 147
Pyrenees 120
Pythagoras 140

Qatar 128
queen of the south. *See* Queen of
  Sheba
Queen of Sheba 48, 53, 167
  gifts to King Solomon 48, 148
Qureish 114
Qur'an 39, 111, 118, 143, 155,
  160–165, 179
  revealed to Muhammad 114,
    162–170
  teachings on Jesus 112
  verses of 165

rabbinic literature 99
Rachel 76
racial problems in the South 33
racial theology. *See* theology
Ramadan 163
Ras al-Khaimah 147
Ras-Beirut 138
al-Rashid, Harun 152, 171
Ras Sajr 46
Reagan, Ronald 179

bombing raid ordered by 180
Rechab 160
Redeemer 94
Red Sea 46, 55
refugee camps 181
relics, worship of 115
religions, non-monotheistic 117
Republic 122
resurrection 76
Reu (chart) 43
Revelation, Book of 120, 189
Revolutionary Communist party 177
Rock of Gibralter 136
Roman:
  architecture 55, 147
  army 55
  influence 117, 135
  province of Syria 55
Roman Empire 127, 150
Romans 134, 152
Rosetta Stone 140
ibn-Rushd (abu-al-Walid Muhammad
    ibn-Ahmad ibn-Rushd) 125. *See*
    also Averroës

Sabaeans (Sabeans) 48, 55, 58. *See*
  also Sheba
Sabak 58
Sadat, President Anwar 179
saints, worship of 114
Salah (chart) 43
Salaman (chart) 113
Salat 162. *See also* prayers
salvation 61, 94, 97, 191. *See also*
  eternal salvation
Samaria 184, 189. *See also* Nablus
Samarian hills 46
Samaritan woman 83
Samaritans 83
Samuel, second book of 100
San'a 47. *See also* Uzal
Saracens 152
Sarah 41, 48, 65, 71, 79, 87, 92, 97,
  107, 191
  casts out Hagar and Ishmael 90,
    101
  (chart) 43
  commended by princes of
    Pharaoh 70, 73
  gives birth to Isaac 97, 102
  Hagar returns to 83
  jealousy toward Hagar 78, 85, 98

Sarah (cont.)
  love for Ishmael 96, 101
  marries Abraham 65
  meets Hagar 73
  obeys Abraham 71
  relationship to Hagar 85
Sarai (Iscah) 65, 73, 79. See also Sarah
Sardinia 133
Saudi Arabia 54, 112, 128
Sawm 162
Scripture 61, 87, 97, 110, 133
  abused 97
  references to Arabs 76
Seba. See Sheba
Seir 51. See also Petra
Sela 51
Selfia 46
Seljuk Turks 152, 165
Semites 48, 142
Semitic 55
  cultures 63
  language 63, 156
Semitic Arabs x, 41–58
  descendants of 48
  God's purpose for 94
  See also Arabs
Semitic family 41
Semitic Jews 55. See also Jews
Sephar (Zhafar) 44
Septuagint 43, 48, 187
Serug (chart) 43
Shahadah 162. See also faith
Shakespeare, William 177
Shamir, Yitzhak 179
Sharjah 147
Sharon, Ariel 184
Sheba 48, 58
  gold of 48
  kingdom of 48
  Queen of (See Queen of Sheba)
Sheba (son of Jokshan) 48, 58
  (chart) 43
Shechem 48, 69
sheikhs 41
Sheleph (Salafa) 46
  (chart) 43
Shelif (Shulaf) 46
Shem 42, 158
  (chart) 43
  God of 44, 48
  sons of 68, 152
  See also al-Sham

Shibam 46
Shiite Muslim, death as a martyr 179
Shiite sect 94, 117, 138
Shi'ites 117
Shua 58
Shuah 58
Shuah (son of Abraham) 58
  (chart) 55
Shulamite woman 53
Shur 78
Sicily 132
Sidon 131–135
Sidon (son of Canaan) 152
ibn-Sina (Abu Ali al-Hussein ibn-
    Abdallah ibn) 122, 125. See also
    Avicenna
Sinai Peninsula 58, 79
Sind ibn-Ali 122
Smith, William 58
Socialist Workers party 176
Sodom 97
Solomon, King 48, 53, 117, 133
  gifts to 48, 148
Solomon, Song of 53
Son of Man 61
Soncino Chumash 73
Sophir (Sophira) 48
Spain 117, 126, 135, 150
  Muslim 124
  ruled by the Arabs 120, 128, 150
  trade with 133
  See also Muslin Spain
Spanish, Arab characteristics of 130
Spanish music 130, 168
"Spartacus" 55
Sphinx 70, 141
Spirit of adoption 87
Spirit of Christ 187
spiritual blindness 184
Stephen 65
Strait of Gibraltar 133
Strait of Hormuz 147
Sudan 128
Suez Canal 147
suffering 70, 92
Sumer 63
Sumerians 63, 152
  tablets 147
Summerian-Akkadian bilingual
    dictionary 158
Sunnites 117
Su'udi Arabia 43

Sychar 83
Syria 48–53, 68, 128, 153
  ancient 152
  Roman province of 55
  under French rule 153
Syrian Desert 53
Syrians 51, 133
Syro-Chaldaeans 51
Syrophoenician woman 130

Tadmor. *See* Palmyra
Tahafut al-Falāsifah 125
Tahafut al-Tahafut 125
tanbur 168
Taper, Bernard 31
Targum 76
Tariq's mountain 134
Tarshish 133. *See also* Spain
Tarsus 120
Tartessus. *See* Cadiz
televangelists 76, 108, 177, 181
Tema (Tayma) 53
  (chart) 50
Temple of Jupiter 55
tentmaking 145
Terah 66
  (chart) 43, 113
terrorism 177–191
  by Arabs and Jews 177–181
  Christian response to 181
  derived from 177
  encountered by foreign powers 181
  government's function in 191
  in Latin America 177
  in Lebanon 179
  in Palestine 177
  reasons for 177
  solution to 181, 188
terrorist 177
  acts in America 177
  anti-American 179
  goal of 177
  Jewish 177–179
Tertullian 118, 147
theology 122, 145
  center of 118
  racial 107
theophanies. *See* God, appearances
    to Hagar
Tigris 51, 63, 158, 171
Tigris-Euphrates Valley 150
Torah 41

Tower of Babel 150
trade routes 48
traditions 53, 76
tribes 48. *See also* Arab tribes
trigonometry 120
Trinity 105, 163
  Second Person of 105
Tripoli 182
Troas 120
tsachāq 97
Tunisia 126, 135
Turkey 120, 152
Turkish Empire 152
Turks. *See* Ottoman Turks
typology 81
Tyre 130–135

Ud (oud) (musical instrument) 168
Ud (chart) 113
Udub (chart) 113
Udub (chart) 113
Um-al-Quaiwain 147
Umayyad caliphs 149–154, 165
United Arab Emirates 148
United Nations Security Council 179
United States:
  and the Middle East 181
  support of Israel 181
  terrorists 179
  terrorizes Muslim villages 179
U.S. News and World Report 177
universal Church. *See* Church
Ur 41, 63–67, 78, 158. *See also* Iraq
Uriah 99
Uz 48
Uzal (Awzal) 46
  (chart) 43
  See also San'a

Valentino, Rudolf 168
Verdi, Guiseppe 142
Viceroy of Egypt. *See* Ismail, Khedive
Visigoth 128

Wadi-el-Qudeirat 78
Ibn-El-Wardee 46
Washington, George 182
Western Christians xv, 173, 181
Westerners, image of Arabs 128
Western political theology 76, 100,
    175
  support of Israel 181

Whiston, William 41
wives, sterile 85, 97
Wycliffe Bible Commentary 97

Yahweh 107
Yaman district 58
Yarub (chart) 113
Yashjub (chart) 113
Yebreen 58
Yehudi 40
Yemen 43–48, 128
Yensu'ah desert 58
Yohai, R. Simon b. 74
Young's Analytical Concordance to the
    Bible 97

Zabram. See Zimran
Zafari 46

Zaid (chart) 113
Zakat 162. See also alms
zambra 171
Zanzibar 152
al-Zarnūji 165
Zenobia, Queen 168
Zerah 48
ziggurat 63
Zilpah 76
Zimran 54
    (chart) 55
Zionism 182, 189
ibn Ziyad, Tariq 136
Zobah 152
Zubaydah 171
Zuwayla Bab 145

Scripture Index

Genesis, Midrash Rabbah—pp. 107, 74

Genesis
1:16—p. 45
1:26—p. 89
1:28—p. 75
1:28—p. 95
2:10-12—p. 49
4:8—p. 176
9:1—p. 95
9:1—p. 75
9:7—p. 75
9:7—p. 95
9:26—p. 48
10:1—p. 40
10:4—p. 134
10:6—p. 44
10:15—p. 133
10:18—p. 152
10:22—pp. 40, 67, 152
10:24—p. 40
10:25—p. 40
10:26-29—pp. 42, 49, 58
10:30—p. 42
10:32—p. 95
11:16-26—p. 42
11:29—p. 66
11:31—p. 66
11:32—p. 68
12:3—p. 38
12:4—p. 69
12:5—p. 69
12:7—p. 69
12:8—p. 69
12:9—p. 66
12:10—p. 70
12:10-20—p. 77
12:15—p. 71

12:17—pp. 65, 73
12:19—p. 72
12:20—p. 75
13:2—p. 73
14:13—p. 41
14:14—pp. 78, 91
15:2—p. 77
15:4—pp. 85, 91
16—pp. 62, 78
16-21—p. 102
16:1—p. 74
16:2—pp. 75, 76
16:3—p. 65
16:4—p. 84
16:6—p. 85
16:7—p. 79
16:8—pp. 80, 89
16:9—pp. 81, 110
16:10—pp. 75, 86, 95, 105, 112, 127
16:11—p. 87
16:12—pp. 46, 87
16:13—p. 89
16:14—p. 79
16:15—p. 89
16:16—p. 90
17:1—p. 91
17:15—p. 66
17:18—p. 91
17:19—p. 91
17:19-21—p. 95
17:20—pp. 51, 75, 82, 95, 105, 112, 125, 148
17:20—pp. 88, 127
17:23—p. 92
18:1—p. 91
18:1-8—p. 97
18:12—p. 72
18:14—p. 75

18:20—p. 97
19—p. 97
20:2—p. 47
20:2-6—p. 77
20:12—p. 65
20:18—p. 65
21:4—p. 97
21:8—p. 97
21:10—p. 99
21:11—p. 103
21:12—p. 103
21:12—p. 104
21:13—pp. 95, 105, 112, 125
21:14—pp. 104, 125
21:17-18—p. 105
21:18—p. 88
21:18—pp. 81, 95, 112
21:18-21—p. 107
21:20—p. 141
21:21—pp. 44, 79, 107
23:19—p. 91
24:2—p. 78
24:10—p. 67
25:1—p. 56
25:2—p. 58
25:3—p. 56
25:6—pp. 48, 56
25:9—p. 107
25:13-15—p. 58
25:14—p. 53
25:18—p. 89
26:1—p. 47
26:1-11—p. 77
28:2—p. 67
28:5—p. 67
28:9—p. 52
29:35—p. 41
36:9—p. 52
36:33—p. 49
37:36—p. 57
38:2—p. 58
38:12—p. 58
41:45—p. 161
50:20—p. 85

Exodus
2:21—p. 161
20:12—p. 65

Leviticus
19:3—p. 65
24:20—p. 138

Numbers
13:6—p. 161

Deuteronomy
11:29—p. 47
27:4—p. 47
27:13—p. 47

Joshua
8:30-33—p. 47
15:21—p. 53
15:52—p. 53
24:2—pp. 42, 63

Judges
9:22—p. 47

2 Samuel
11—p. 71

1 Kings
9:28—p. 48
10:1-10—p. 48
10:10—p. 149
10:11—p. 49
11:14-25—p. 54

2 Kings
14:7—p. 51

1 Chronicles
1:20-23—pp. 49, 58
1:22—p. 47
1:29-32—p. 58
2:3—p. 58

Job
1:1—p. 49
6:19—p. 54

Psalms
34:4—p. 106
34:6—p. 106
72:15—p. 49
103:14—p. 65
105:23—p. 44
106:22—p. 44

Proverbs
22:6—p. 82
30:1—p. 54
31:1—p. 54

Song of Songs
1:5—p. 52
3:6—p. 149

Isaiah
13:12—p. 48
16:1—p. 52
21:11—p. 53
21:13–17—p. 52
21:14—p. 54
35:2—p. 136
55:89—p. 65
60:7—p. 51
63:1—p. 51

Jeremiah
1:7b–10—p. 34
1:7b–17—p. 34
22:23—p. 136
25:24—p. 41
29:13—p. 106

Ezekiel
27:21—p. 52

Daniel
4:17—p. 109
4:35—p. 109

Hosea
2:14—p. 79

Habakkuk
p. 61

Zechariah
4:10—p. 107

Matthew
2:1—p. 161
5:44—pp. 138, 190
10:27—p. 163
11:28—p. 87
12:42—p. 48
13:24–30—p. 67
15:26–28—p. 131
23:37—p. 82
27:46—p. 68
28:19—p. 184

Mark
7:13—p. 95
10:29–30—p. 35
15:34—p. 68
16:15—p. 184

Luke
3:1–2—p. 55
19:10—pp. 60, 87
19:10—p. 72
19:13—p. 136
24:47—p. 184

John
1:18—p. 61
1:29—p. 109
4:14—p. 82
4:24—p. 61
4:28–39—p. 82
4:42—p. 70
8:56–58—p. 70
10:3—p. 81
12:27—p. 68
15:5—p. 92
15:14—p. 69
17:20–26—p. 185

Acts
1:8—p. x
2:11—p.
4:18—p. 184
7:2—pp. 42, 69
7:2–3—p. 64
8:1–3—p. 186
10:35—pp. 63, 99
11:26—p. 152
13:14—p. 152
16:14—p.
17:11—p. xvi
17:21—p. 53
17:26–31—p. 95
17:31—p. 86
19:32—p. 185
19:39—p. 186
19:41—p. 186

Romans
1:16—p. 184
2:29—p. 92
3:11—p. 87
4:11—p. 92
5:9—p. 93

8:9—p. 186
8:15—p. 87
8:28—p. 73
10:17—p. 70
11:33—p. 61
12:1—p. 86
12:14—p. 190
12:17—p. 190
12:19—p. 190
13:1—p. 190
15:4—p. 88

I Corinthians
1:27-29—p. 61
10:11—p. 88
12:13—p. 186

Ephesians
3:6—p. 186
3:9—p. 186
6:1-3—p. 65

Philippians
3:8-10—p. 138
3:10—p. 75
3:20—p. 189

I Timothy
2:1-3—p. 190

2 Timothy
4:7-8—p. 191

Titus
2:14—p. v

Hebrews
2:3—p. 189
4:12—p. 65

4:13—p. 85
9:22—p. 92
11:8—p. 69
12:5-6—p. 73
12:7—p. 92

James
2:23—pp. 69, 72
4:6—p. 86

I Peter
3:4-6—p. 72
5:7—p. 62

2 Peter
1:20-21—p. 99
3:9—p. 188
3:9—p. 95

I John
1:9—p. 81
4:12—p. 61

3 John
5-8—p. 38

Jude
3—p. 118

Revelation
3:16—pp. 82, 115
4:11—p. 91
7:9-10—p. 191
13:8—pp. 79, 188
14:11—p. 188
17:8—p. 79
17:17—p. 110

About the Author

Louis Bahjat Hamada was born to an aristocratic Lebanese family in Hawran (biblical Haran), a southwestern district of Syria, where his father served as prosecutor general under the French mandatory rule. After the untimely death of his parents, Hamada was reared in Lebanon by his grandfather, who was the head of the Druze religion, an outgrowth of Islam.

Hamada came to the U.S. in 1953 and was converted to faith in Christ on September 11, 1955. Since then, he has earned a Ph.D. in music education from Florida State University and a Master's degree from Dallas Theological Seminary. He is an ordained minister of the gospel and a noted international Bible teacher. Hamada is also a recognized authority on Semitic Arabs and Muslim evangelization. He is the executive director of a faith ministry: the Hamada Evangelistic Outreach, Inc.

Dr. Hamada was officially inducted into the Oxford Society of Scholars on July 17, 1987, based on his "excellence in research related to problem-solving within the family, community, and church and contributing to knowledge potentially enhancing the growth of Christianity."

Dr. Hamada now has a traveling ministry of preaching, teaching, and equipping Christians to understand and reach out in love to the Arabs and Muslims. Grieved over unfortunate misconceptions and misconstrued interpretations of biblical truths that many Christians have about the Arabs, Dr. Hamada helps believers understand biblical texts such as Genesis 12:3, the accounts of Hagar and Ishmael, and Galatians 4:30.

In addition to his worldwide evangelistic ministry, Dr. Hamada teaches short-term courses at several Christian institutions, such as Columbia Bible College and Seminary, Covenant College, Washington Bible College, and the School of Intercultural Studies at Biola University. He also conducts educational tours to the Middle East in collaboration with the Zwemer Institute of Muslim Studies.

Dr. Hamada may be contacted for speaking engagements at the following address:

Dr. Louis Hamada
P.O. Box 3333
Jackson, TN 38303
(901) 668-8350